ANGER-FREE

ANGER-FREE

TEN BASIC STEPS
TO MANAGING YOUR ANGER

W. Doyle Gentry, Ph.D.

QUILL
An Imprint of HarperCollins*Publishers*

HarperCollins books may be purchased for educational, business, or sales promotional use. For information please write: Special Markets Department, HarperCollins Publishers Inc., 10 East 53rd Street, New York, NY 10022.

First Quill edition published 2000.

Book design by Michael Mendelsohn at MM Design 2000, Inc.

Library of Congress Cataloging-in-Publication Data has been applied for.

ISBN 0-688-15500-6
ISBN 0-688-17587-2 (pbk.)

05 06 07 08 09   20 19 18 17 16 15 14 13 12

To

Andrew C. Bockner, M.D.

for believing in me when I could
no longer believe in myself

ACKNOWLEDGMENTS

I could not have completed this awesome journey without the help of others. First, I want to thank the contributors to the 1995 ASJA/APA symposium for mental health professionals, especially Guy B. Kettelhack, for providing concrete "how to" advice for turning a good idea into something publishable. Second, and most important, I am forever indebted to William Morrow's Toni Sciarra for taking a chance on an unknown, albeit promising, author. She opened a door that I have been wanting to walk through my entire life! The gratitude I feel toward my colleague Ken West for his editing of the early draft of this manuscript is immeasurable; if there was a painless way to criticize what I wrote, Ken always found it. And, then there are my many friends—especially Wayne and Sherry Sloop—who sustained their interest and encouragement throughout the two years it took me to complete this project. I thank them for their steadfast loyalty. I am grateful, as well, to a second member of the William Morrow team, Katharine Cluverius, for her expert editorial assistance, her intelligent humor, and her constant reassurance; she clearly deserves much of the credit for whatever measure of success this book achieves. There is also my good friend Tom Haney, who served as my link to the many resource materials essential to the writing of the book that were not readily accessible. I am indebted to my early mentors—Jack Hokanson, Charles Spielberger, Edwin Megargee—and later colleagues—Ernest Harburg and Ernest Johnson—whose authoritative research on the topic of anger quite naturally shaped many of the ideas expressed in this book. I am also thankful to many people whose names and identifying characteristics have been altered to protect their privacy, who were willing to share their "anger stories" with me so that I might in turn share them with you. Last, I wish to express my appreciation to Sybil Frey, who laboriously typed and retyped every word in this manuscript and who acted as if she thoroughly enjoyed the task all the while.

A special note of thanks goes to my immediate family—my wife of thirty-two years, Catherine, my two wonderful adult children, Rebecca and Chris, and my faithful bassett hound, Arthur—who bring joy and meaning to each and every day of my life.

CONTENTS

*The best time to manage anger
is before it happens.*
—W.D.G.

CHAPTER 1

SOME VERY ANGRY PEOPLE

My life is in the hands of any
rascal who chooses to annoy me.
—Dr. John Hunter, eighteenth-century physician

John is a sixty-year-old, soon-to-be-retired machinist who has suffered from too much anger his whole adult life. He is a likable man who by all accounts has tried to live a decent life, work hard, and take care of his family. He is an ex-Marine and is proud of having served his country. He pays his bills, attends church regularly, and helps his neighbors when he can. He is ordinary in all respects but one, and that is his extraordinary temper.

"Were you always this angry?" I asked.

"Oh, yes. When I was a kid, I had a violent temper. I've got scars on my head from hammers. I'd get angry when I mashed my finger and throw the hammer straight up in the air. It'd come back down and hit me right on top of my head."

John was clearly the victim of his own anger.

"What did your anger feel like?" I asked.

"Like I was gonna explode . . . on whoever or whatever was around me. I could feel myself tensing up inside, getting ready to go off. I'd actually see stars," he said.

"And afterward, how did you feel?" I asked.

"Drained! It takes a lot of energy out of you. I was afraid I was going to have a stroke or heart attack—my blood pressure couldn't stand it. I think I got a hiatal hernia from being so angry. And you can't rest; you just toss and tumble."

John remembers first becoming angry when he began public school. Up until then, he didn't think of himself as an angry person. "Our family moved into a neighborhood where everybody was cousin-this and cousin-that and we were outsiders. They picked on us, and we had to take up for ourselves. You fought for everything you got." He's still fighting fifty years later.

♦ ♦ ♦

Brian is twenty-nine. He is married, has four young children, and is a welder. He goes to college part-time. To look at him, you wouldn't think there was anything wrong with him, but he too suffers from too much anger. Although Brian feels bad about his angry outbursts, he also feels relief.

"Afterward, I feel more relaxed. I guess with it [anger] boiling over, it gets it out of my system."

"Can you control your anger at all?" I asked.

"No. It doesn't build up slowly. It just comes on all of a sudden. Like a switch is thrown. My level of anger rises from zero to the highest point it can, just that quick."

Like John, Brian also had a bad temper as a child. His mother would tell him, "If people push you, you need to walk away." But he would get mad and end up fighting instead.

Brian is most apt to get angry if he feels mistreated or in situations in which he feels helpless, and he tends to dwell on his anger, sometimes for days. "I wouldn't be mad all that time, but I would sit and think about it for a couple of hours at a time."

Brian doesn't come from an angry family, so he doesn't understand why he's always had trouble with his temper. He doesn't like being so angry, and he realizes that his anger is out of proportion to what other people might feel in the same situation. "Where another person gets a little upset, I'm angry!"

♦ ♦ ♦

Rachel is forty-two, divorced, and the mother of two grown children. She cried as we talked about how anger has affected her life. "There was so much I wanted to do, but anger at the way my life was going kept me from doing those things. My anger hurt me. It kept me from having things that people I grew up with had, like a college education and a good job."

Like the others, Rachel had been angry since childhood. "Nobody fooled with me. I had an attitude." She had been raised in an alcoholic, abusive family, and she had learned to defend herself by staying angry and fighting back at the world.

For Rachel, anger was a defense against a backlog of emotional problems that she constantly tried to hide and that she had never confronted. She thought, "If I don't talk about it—the hurt, the pain, the abuse—I can put it back on this little shelf." But these problems were repeatedly expressed through self-abuse and the abuse of those closest to her.

Sometimes Rachel's anger is so strong that "swallowing it" and getting away from the angry situation isn't enough. At this point, she has to express her anger by throwing things or slamming doors. Her whole life has been a struggle, one that brought her to me feeling guilty, depressed, alienated from loved ones, and full of regret.

♦ ♦ ♦

David is fifty-five. He's in constant pain from a twenty-year-old work injury, which left him permanently unemployed. Repeated back surgery and years of medical treatment have failed to relieve his pain, leaving him a frustrated and very angry man. "The more pain I have, the madder I get. Simple things, stupid things, set me off, like watching my family having a good time when I can't or watching them rake leaves and not being able to help."

David's family has had to bear the brunt of his angry outbursts. "I

I'm not sure what set me off, but there I was with the refriger-ator door open and a large jar of mayonnaise in my hand. All of a sudden I exploded with anger. My heart was beating so hard I could feel it, and blood was rushing around my eyes into my temples. I felt an urge to do something with all this emotion, but what?

I looked at my wife, Catherine, standing a few feet away, a hor-rified expression on her face, gasping, "Doyle," and I thought about throwing the jar at her. I honestly think it would have killed her. Then I looked at the glass doors leading off from the kitchen, and I thought about throwing it at them. What an explosion that would have made.

Finally, I just threw the damn thing down on the floor as hard as I could. It made a sound you wouldn't have believed. Mayonnaise and glass went everywhere, but at that moment I felt absolutely exhilarated! The whole episode was over in seconds, and I was calm again.

can tell when he's angry," his daughter says, "and I just go to my room. I don't want to make him any madder than he already is." The whole family tries their best to dance around his anger. "We all know what to do and what not to do," his daughter explains.

David is full of regret about being so angry, but knowing he hurts his family does not help. David still gets angry. "It's hard to explain. It just builds up over a period of time, and I've just got to let it out!"

David feels hopeless and defeated by his anger. He's tried everything to control it. "I've tried going off by myself. I've cried. I've hollered and screamed. I've burned things, hit things, smashed things . . . none of it helped. It just cost me in the long run. I'm always sorry afterward, but it's too late. I see tears in my wife's eyes, but it's too late."

Too much anger, in fact, almost cost David his life: It caused him to have a heart attack seven years ago.

♦ ♦ ♦

I met Dennis when I was working at Duke University Medical School about twenty years ago. He had been admitted to our psychiatric inpatient service, and I was asked to do a diagnostic consultation on him. Dennis was in his late forties, and he had risen from the rank of accountant to president of a rather large company in record time. He was a driven, take-charge kind of guy who suddenly found himself extremely depressed, lacking in energy and initiative, and feeling worthless.

I remember our first meeting. I came to interview him just as he was leaving to go to his biofeedback class. He was in a hurry to get there so that he could show the instructor that he could "relax more than any of those other patients." As we walked briskly along, I asked him how he felt about being in a psychiatric facility. He stopped abruptly, put his arm on my shoulder, looked straight at me and said, "Son, that's a stupid f—— question, don't you think?" He smiled and went running off down the hall.

Dennis was quickly returning to his former "Type A" self. His depression, which was beginning to lift, had only suppressed his usual cynical, hostile disposition. Underneath it all, David remained a very angry man.

♦ ♦ ♦

These people all suffer from a common problem: *toxic, unhealthy, maladaptive* anger. By current estimate, at least 20 million Americans suffer from "toxic anger." You yourself may be one of these people. For almost fifty years, I was, but I am not anymore.

When does anger become toxic? When you get angry too often? When your anger is too intense? When it lasts too long? When it negatively affects your life? Some experts say you should "hold your anger in," whereas others tell you to "let it out." Who's right? And what can be done to solve the problems caused by toxic anger? This book answers all of these questions. *Anger-Free* provides a simple self-assessment method of identifying toxic anger, addresses the psychobiological influ-

My father was a passionate man, and sometimes that passion turned into anger.

I remember a time he took the family out to dinner at a local drive-in restaurant. He started out in a good mood since he had gotten paid that day and had stopped on the way home to have a couple of beers, and he seemed to be enjoying us kids despite our ceaseless chatter in the front seat of the pickup truck.

But all of that soon changed. It took a long time to get our order (probably because it was so large), and I could see my father getting upset about waiting. The tension in his face and raised tone of his voice signaled that something bad was about to happen.

When the young girl finally arrived with the food and set it on a tray attached to the car window, he said angrily, "We don't want the damn food. Take it back." When she told him he would have to pay anyway, he threw some money on the tray and then threw the tray as hard as he could across the parking lot. The girl started crying and everyone around us looked on in a state of shock. We waited the rest of the night for his anger to subside.

ences that bring a person to the point of anger, outlines the seven major disincentives for remaining too angry, and offers a basic ten-step program for "detoxifying" this potentially harmful emotion.

EXERCISE

ARE YOU AN ANGRY PERSON?

1. Take out a pad and pencil and write out your own anger story. When did you first become an angry person? What sort of things make you angry? How intense is your anger? Does it last long? How do you generally express it? What are the consequences of your anger for your mental and

physical health, relationships, and so on? Do you feel that anger has been an asset or a liability in your life?

2. Ask yourself how you feel after writing these thoughts about your anger. Are you relieved or do you feel uneasy? Are you sad? Did you become angry doing the activity? Do you feel as if you are unlocking secrets from your past?

3. Does what you wrote surprise you? Would you feel comfortable sharing these thoughts with someone else? Why or why not?

CHAPTER 2

TOXIC ANGER SYNDROME

*Anger, though a vital ingredient in
individual and social life,
is inherently a somewhat elusive emotion.
No group or society can encourage a
fully free indulgence in anger.*

—Carol Stearns, M.D., Ph.D., and Peter Stearns, Ph.D.,
Anger: The Struggle for Emotional Control in America's History

Drs. Carol and Peter Stearns, psychiatrist and historian, respectively, and authors of the provocative book *Anger: The Struggle for Emotional Control in America's History,* must have anticipated the problem of toxic anger when they suggested that no society can allow for the full, uncontrolled, and indiscriminate experience of anger among its citizenry. However, these authors also aptly point out that the suppression of anger historically has led to an increasing ambivalence about anger, which ultimately endangers the very essence of our social, family, work, and religious lives. What the Stearns advocate, in effect, is a genuine freedom both to experience and to express a reasonable and healthy degree of anger in the course of everyday human interaction, the key words being *reasonable* and *healthy*.

Where do we draw the line? How much anger is enough? How much is too much? And what solutions do we offer people whose anger has become toxic? Our failure to address such questions on both a theoretical and a practical level has resulted in what the Stearns call society's "disingenuous" attitude toward anger:

> We are told, by people who should know better, that we live in an age of emotional liberation, one in which . . . the damaging forces of age-old repressions can be identified and reversed. This is not the case. The modern impulse to tolerate wider emotional expression is highly selective; it carefully excludes anger. Perhaps we are freer to express tenderness, or sexual passion, or fear, than our ancestors were. . . . But tolerance of anger is declining, not increasing, and the pretense of emotional liberation should not serve, as it has to date, as a smoke screen for this fact.[1]

This exact point was brought home to me some years ago when I asked a psychotherapy client, during his first appointment, why he thought he needed help. He replied, "My wife says I don't show enough emotion. She wants me to be a more emotional husband, and her therapist agrees." The man and I worked together for several months, achieving some success in exploring his emotions and the reasons behind his restraint. One day he asked if he could bring his wife to the next session. I said that was fine, so she came with him the following week. His wife, it turned out, had come to complain that she was unhappy about her husband's treatment. Specifically, she was upset that he had become openly (and uncharacteristically) angry with her on several recent occasions—not rageful, but clearly angry. "But I thought you asked your husband to get help so he could be more emotional," I said. In response she jumped up and shouted, "I only want him to show positive emotions! He can keep his anger to himself!" and stormed out of my office.

♦ ♦ ♦

Along with disgust, fear, joy, sadness, and surprise, anger is one of six basic emotions recognized worldwide by cultures that range from West-

I remember once Catherine got so angry at me that she spent the whole day swinging a pickax, digging up our hard Virginia soil for a flower garden we had been talking about putting in for years. We had put the project off, both of us, because quite frankly we didn't have the energy to tackle it. But that day, she was one "energized" woman! God knows what she was thinking as she swung that ax with all her might. That evening, after her energy was all spent, we talked about what I had done to provoke such anger, and I vowed to try and change my behavior. And eight years later, we still have a bed of beautiful daylilies.

ern societies to tribes in New Guinea and Borneo.[2] There are many positive functions of anger in everyday life: It energizes behavior, it serves as a catalyst for resolving interpersonal conflict, it promotes self-esteem, and it fosters a sense of personal control during times of peak stress.[3] However, this book is not about helping people learn to ventilate anger to achieve such outcomes or to improve their health.[4] It's certainly not about people like Carla and Tom who experience normal, nontoxic anger.

I have known Carla for more than thirty years. I have rarely seen her angry. "I get more frustrated than angry," she said when I interviewed her. "I can't remember the last time I really got angry." Although she admits she feels a little tense when she gets mad, she has never been so angry that she "sees stars." Her anger is over quickly, and she never dwells on it. Anger does not dominate her life.

Tom is a longtime friend too in his fifties, and someone whom I have not seen angry often. "I get angry maybe three or four times a year," he says. Tom's easygoing temperament, along with his Quaker upbringing, makes it difficult for him to get mad at most things. "Don't get me wrong, I have been so angry at times, like during my divorce, that I had this tremendous urge to hurt someone, but I didn't." The opposing feeling of "not wanting to hurt someone" was too strong to let him harm anyone.

Hostility is like the stain that is left behind when tea sits too long in a cup. The inside of the cup is discolored forever and a bitter taste remains. That's what happens when we sit on anger too long; it discolors our view of the world. What was once friendly is now unfriendly. What once was kind is now unkind. Those who were on our side are now against us. Hostility is the residue of unexpressed anger. It makes us lose our taste for life!

His anger too is short-lived. "I get my head together and decide what I want to do about the situation, do it, and when it's done, so's the anger."

This book is not about annoyance. Annoyance does not involve the element of blame typical of anger; it is less often motivated by a desire for revenge; and it is less likely to be experienced within the context of a negative mood state such as depression.[5] Finally, this book is not focused on hostility and aggression. Although anger clearly has some connection with hostility and aggressive behavior, it is not the same.[6] Hostility is an *attitude* of ill will, aggression refers to *behavior* that is always meant to hurt, whereas anger is an *emotion*. By failing to appreciate the meaningful distinction between anger and these other concepts, we misunderstand the uniqueness of the anger experience and the role it plays in our everyday lives.

This book is about what I call the *toxic anger syndrome* (TAS). TAS is defined by a level of anger that is experienced by otherwise normal people much too frequently, is too intense, and lasts too long. It is more than mere annoyance and different from positive, adaptive anger. By *adaptive* I mean anger that optimizes our ability not only to survive physically but, more important, to do so in a healthy and harmonious fashion with those around us. Moreover, the term *syndrome* suggests a pattern of destructive consequences that, in my clinical experience, always result from toxic anger. *When it comes to toxic anger, there is no free ride. Its costs can be measured economically, socially, vocationally, mentally, and physically!*

I believe, as do a growing number of other psychologists, that TAS will one day receive official recognition by the American Psychiatric Association in its *Diagnostic and Statistical Manual of Mental Disorders* and will no longer be thought of simply as a symptom of various other mood and personality disorders. It is my hope that this book and the help that it brings to those who read it will further that end.

◆ ◆ ◆

Through my research studies and years of observing anger-prone patients, I have defined ten unique characteristics of TAS, described in the following sections.

FREQUENCY, INTENSITY, AND DURATION

TAS involves a type of angry reaction that is distinguished from both annoyance and normal, nontoxic anger by its frequency, intensity, and/or duration. It is important to note that people need not suffer from all three of these dimensions of toxic anger to qualify as suffering from TAS. For example, Jeffrey is nineteen years old. He is liked by most people who know him and is typically regarded as easygoing. Few things make him angry. When he does get mad, the mood is usually over about as soon as it begins. However, on rare occasions he gets so angry that he is his own worst enemy. For example, he was once playing basketball in a recreational league and he missed an easy layup. He got so mad that he smashed his hand into the brick wall behind the basket and ended up with a compound fracture that required complicated surgery and cost his parents more than a thousand dollars. A big price tag for one moment of intense anger!

Or there is the case of Reuben's parents: Reuben initially came to me wanting help in dealing with midlife depression. When I asked him how his parents had dealt with their anger (thinking about potential role models in Reuben's life for handling anger), he replied, "I don't ever recall either of them being angry." I found it incredible that he had lived with these two people for more than twenty years and had never once seen them angry. He then recalled that even though they did not get angry, they would frequently disagree "and then not speak a word to each other for weeks at a time."

Jeffrey's problem is one of intensity, not frequency or duration. Reuben's parents' anger, on the other hand, is not especially intense but is too frequent and lasts too long. Neither case involves normal anger, and both clearly have negative consequences. Jeffrey had to deal with his parents' anger over his self-inflicted medical problem (not to mention the expense, which they rightfully passed on to him), and Reuben grew up in a climate of hostile silence and parental alienation, which served as a breeding ground for the depression he suffered later in life.

PHYSICAL EXPRESSION

TAS involves a type of anger that invariably demands some form of physical expression. Sometimes this involves an overt, "public" expression of aggressive behavior. Remember John from Chapter 1? He ended up with scars on his head from throwing hammers when he got outraged. Rachel once got so angry that she hit her son in the face with a pitchfork. Dennis didn't get physically aggressive when he got angry at me but simply let me know (with a smile) that I had asked a "stupid f___ question"!

Far more of the time, however, anger finds a "private" means of physically expressing itself. Dr. James Averill, a psychologist at the University of Massachusetts, found that as few as 10 percent of angry people "act out" in some overtly aggressive manner.[7] The vast majority are what anger researchers and therapists describe as "anger suppressors," or "anger-in" type personalities. What is suppressed, however, is not the anger itself but the overt aggressive reaction that usually accompanies extreme anger. *It is a fallacy to think that rage can be harmlessly and effectively suppressed!* Where does it go? Nowhere. Anger stays inside the mind and body, converting itself into hostility, depression, ulcers, high blood pressure, heart disease, bruxism (grinding one's teeth), musculoskeletal pain, cancer, psoriasis, and headaches. These are two examples.

The wife of a friend of mine called late one night, asking that I come to her house immediately. Her husband, she said, was in the backyard screaming and beating a rake against a tree. She had never seen him so angry! I asked her, "Would you rather take him to the emergency room?" She said no and asked what that had to do with his ranting and raving. I reminded her that her husband was quite overweight, had a history of high blood pressure, had heart disease in his family, and lately had been under a lot of stress at work. I said that if he tried to contain all that anger right now, he'd most likely start having chest pain and could be a candidate for a heart attack. Besides, I told her, he can't hurt that big tree with the rake, and if he breaks the rake, so what? With his new promotion, he can afford to buy a dozen rakes. "But what will our neighbors think?" she said. "I don't know," I said, "but is it worth risking a heart attack? When someone's as angry as George is, it's got to go somewhere!"

I gave her one final bit of advice: "I wouldn't get between George and the tree right now. It could be dangerous."

Charles initially wanted help dealing with grief over the loss of his wife. He was a highly educated man in his early sixties, soft-spoken, and not at all a hostile-looking individual. He was a Southern gentleman from the old school who had avoided confrontation all of his life, preferring instead to keep quiet if someone offended him in any way. During the day, he would always say that things were okay when they were not, and he would allow friends and strangers to take advantage of his good nature. He denied himself any feeling other than occasional frustration or slight irritation. But at night, Charles was less able to control his anger. Suffering from severe bruxism, he broke many of his teeth over the years grinding them at night. On one occasion, he awoke to find blood all over his bedsheets and three teeth shattered beyond repair. That cost him fifteen hundred dollars! Charles was full of toxic anger; he just didn't know it.

Aaron, a young man in his thirties, had an interesting way of expressing his all-too-frequent rage. When he got angry, he would chew on the inside of his mouth until it was raw and bleeding. The angrier he became, the more he chewed. Sometimes, it got to the point that his face was so swollen he had to drink out of a straw and could hardly talk. Most of the time, he wasn't aware he was doing it. When I asked him if he was angry about something, he said, "No, I don't know why I do this. But it's been a problem since I was a little boy." Aaron didn't like to get angry because his father had always been angry and at times abusive. Aaron always tried to be reasonable and keep his feelings to himself.

Anger can also cause one to engage unwittingly and excessively in various "health risk" behaviors including ingesting legal, but potentially lethal, substances such as fatty foods, nicotine, alcohol, and caffeine. People try to eat, drink, and smoke away their rage. In addition, anger can lead to auto accidents, work injuries, workaholism, and other destructive behavior.

DEFENSIVENESS

TAS is seen principally in highly defensive individuals. Although it is true that all emotions by their nature act as biological and psychological safeguards to ensure our survival, it is also true that some of us are more endowed with these so-called defenses than others. The capacity to experience anger is at least partially programmed into us genetically. This biological basis for emotionality is referred to as *temperament,* which for the most part is unchanging throughout our lives (see Chapter 4). The capacity to experience anger is, however, also partially learned. John learned to be angry as a way of protecting himself from other youngsters who treated him as an outsider. Rachel learned to be angry not only as a way to defend herself from further physical and emotional abuse, but also as a means of sealing off other painful emotions such as fear and sadness. Dennis learned to be angry as a way of coercing others into doing what he wanted or dismissing them when, in his estimation, they proved foolish and incompetent.

EARLY BEGINNINGS

TAS usually begins to manifest itself early in life. For many of you, anger is a by-product of exposure to parents who themselves suffered from TAS, and who passed it on to you as your earliest and most influential role models for emotionality and coping.

A woman once brought her twelve-year-old son to see me because he was, she said, "angry all the time, disobedient, and destructive." She and her husband were apparently at their wits' end as to how to control their son. They had tried punishment. They had tried rewarding him when he acted civilly. Nothing worked! So she sought professional help. Some weeks into treatment, as I was talking with her about whether her son was showing any sign of change at home, she happened to mention that things had been going much better until the other night, when her son did something that made her husband mad. The boy had not turned down a radio he was playing when his father told him to, at which point his father jumped up, got red in the face, grabbed the radio, threw it on the floor, stomped on it until it broke into a million pieces, and then yelled, "Now let's hear you play the damn radio!" Suddenly I knew why the boy was so angry—he had a good teacher!

Moreover, many people who suffer from TAS are exposed early in life to situations that put them on the defensive and keep them there long enough for their anger to develop *a life of its own,* independent of the changing nature of their life circumstances. This was certainly true of John, Brian, and Dennis, whose early angry, aggressive struggles became lifelong bad habits. Anger for these folks was a type of "character armor" that had served them well in their early years but, as they grew older, left them feeling increasingly drained and weary.

AN INTERNAL PROBLEM

TAS is an internal problem that is not caused, and thus cannot be "fixed," by the actions of others. Many people repeatedly get angry or hang on to their angry feelings too long because they mistakenly believe that the solution to their toxic anger lies outside of themselves in the actions of others. Angry people are forever saying, "He made me so mad!" But they're wrong.

A young woman came to me for help with stress management. Her job as a waitress was literally tormenting her. To illustrate what she had to deal with each day, she told me about a situation that had occurred the night before, involving two customers. Customer A had brought his family in for dinner just before the evening rush, had gotten served, and (when things were the busiest) began hollering in an increasingly loud voice, "Miss, could I please have more coffee over here!" and "This coffee's cold, I want some hot coffee!" and "What do I have to do to get some service around here!" No matter what she did to please him (and his embarrassed family), nothing seemed to satisfy his anger. At the same time, Customer B had come in with his whole family—children, grandchildren, about ten in all—to celebrate his sixtieth birthday. They were laughing and enjoying each other's company when the waitress returned with their orders and proceeded to trip and fall, spilling all the food in Customer B's lap. She fell on the floor and for a minute lay there, afraid to get up for fear that everyone would be angry with her. Instead, Customer B reached down, helped her to her feet, and (with food all over his suit and tie) laughed and said, "Actually, I wanted this steak well done." No one was upset or angry after all!

The moral of the story? Customer A is an angry man, plain and simple. Customer B is not. Nothing that occurred in the restaurant that evening had anything to do with how either of them felt.

How often have you said of someone you know, "They make me so angry, I could . . ."? If you have, like Customer A you are "externalizing" your anger.

SPONTANEOUS, UNREASONABLE, AND UNCONTROLLABLE

TAS involves a type of anger that is often spontaneous, unreasonable, and uncontrollable. There's a bumper sticker I like that says "S___ happens!" The same is true of anger. Anger happens. Most of the time, we experience it suddenly, without warning, and mindlessly. For years, psychologists believed that all emotions resulted from thoughts. You see a bear and you think, "My God, he could kill me!" Then you begin to feel afraid and you run. You see a beautiful woman and you think, "My God, she's beautiful; she's perfect; she's got everything it takes to make me happy!" Then you begin to feel love and you pursue her. But research and science have proved this theory wrong. People are, in fact, "afraid" or "in love" long before they consciously think about what they are doing and why. The rationale for their emotion is typically developed *after the fact*, not before.

PERSONALITY THEMES

Because the level of anger in TAS is disproportionate to the situation in which it is experienced, *TAS most often reflects hidden, unconscious, pathological agendas, or personality "themes" that drive the individual's behavior throughout life.* A middle-aged man who lives in an expensive house and wears thousand-dollar suits angrily assaults his wife two mornings in a row. Why? According to him, on one occasion it was because she was thoughtless enough to "let the kids drink all the orange juice the day before, leaving none for *my* breakfast" and on the next "she left the child's car seat in *my* luxury car." The underlying pathological theme here is an exaggerated sense of entitlement. This man not only feels entitled to a perfect, hassle-free existence, but also feels that his wife should devote all her time and energy each day to ensure that *his* needs are met. This same theme of entitlement holds true to a lesser degree for those

All the time my children were growing up, whenever I heard the two of them arguing or one of them arguing with Catherine, I would find myself getting angry and eventually racing upstairs to put a stop to the argument. All I succeeded in doing, however, was escalating the argument to the point that everyone was hollering, and I was the angriest one of all. Why did I feel this intense, uncontrollable need to intervene in someone else's argument? As my therapist explained my behavior some years ago, "It's not your kids fighting, Doyle, it's your parents all over again. Every time you hear people shouting, an unconscious alarm goes off in you, signaling you to do something you couldn't do as a small child—to rush off and stop these people you love from hurting one another."

Now if I hear them fighting, I just turn up the television or take the dog for a walk. What I cannot hear cannot hurt me or them. At last, people in my family can try to resolve their differences—now that I no longer interfere. It's a win-win solution!

of us who get mad when we have to stand in line at the post office, grocery store, or bank or sit endlessly in traffic. As I will show, entitlement is but one of several pathological themes that characterize people suffering from TAS.

DIFFERENT MOTIVES

TAS serves no specific motive. Dr. Averill's studies have shown that most people are moved to a state of anger by the desire for revenge, the need to accomplish something constructive, or simply to "let off steam." Revenge is a type of *malevolent* anger, the aim of which is to express dislike, to break off a relationship, or to get even for past wrongs. *Constructive* anger, on the other hand, is used to assert authority or independence, to strengthen a relationship, or to get someone to do something for you. The third type of anger, which Averill refers to as *fractious* anger, is simply a response to accumulated frustration—nothing more. Contrary to what you might expect, the most frequently cited type of anger was constructive anger (63 percent of those questioned), followed by revenge (57 percent), and finally anger aimed at "letting off steam" (37 percent).

Again, it is the level of anger that we experience that produces "toxic" consequences, not the reasons behind the anger. For instance, parents who physically abuse their children often are not trying to hurt them.They may simply be trying to get them to behave or to teach them a "constructive" lesson. The harm comes not from the intended lesson but from the intensity of their anger at the moment.

Peter had worked hard all day. When he got home, he was tired and just wanted to relax and watch TV. But this was the night his wife played bridge and he had to take care of their two young children. The evening went well at first; the kids entertained themselves while he relaxed and ate his supper. But then the younger child (who was only fourteen months old) started to cry about something her sister had done to her. Peter told her to stop, that "Daddy is trying to watch TV," but she kept on crying. He told her again, but she still didn't stop and her cries grew louder. Without thinking, he grabbed her by both her arms and shook her as hard as he could, shouting, "I told you to stop crying!" She kept crying, so he kept on shaking her, harder and harder. Peter broke both of his daughter's arms that night, something he was terribly distraught about when his wife returned later that evening and afterward when he finally told the truth to authorities. He was not trying to hurt his child, he said, only to get her to be quiet.

Clearly, more than one motive can simultaneously underlie a person's anger in any given instance. It stands to reason that the more sources of motivation there are, the more toxic the anger. In effect, one is trying to accomplish too much with anger all at once.

> For the first five years that I was depressed, my anger was ma-
> levolent. I wanted to strike out and hurt people. Otherwise, I think
> my anger was mostly constructive. I used anger to make a point or
> to get people to do what I wanted them to do. I remember one
> psychiatrist at Duke who characterized me as "intimidating." I
> couldn't see my behavior then, but looking back, I can. And, unfor-
> tunately, I was the same way at home.

EMOTIONAL DISTRESS

TAS leaves one feeling emotionally distressed and physically drained. The
relief and exhilaration that sometimes accompanies the expression of
toxic anger is short-lived. The long-term psychological ramifications
include feelings of profound regret, guilt, estrangement from anger
"victims," depression, hopelessness, helplessness, self-loathing, and personal defeat. The physical aftermath is characterized by a feeling of "vital
exhaustion."

DOSE-RESPONSE RELATIONSHIP

*A "dose-response" relationship exists between the severity of TAS and its
consequences.* Consider, for example, a recent study by Dr. Ichiro Kawachi and his associates at the Harvard School of Public Health concerning the causes of heart disease.[9] A total of 1,305 men were given a
short test that asked them about their problems controlling anger. The
test was given at a time when the subjects were still healthy, and then
they were followed for seven years. Twenty of these men died of a heart
attack, thirty experienced a nonfatal attack, and sixty others suffered
from angina pectoris, which is persistent chest pain. Forty-three percent
overall scored exceptionally high on the anger measure, and it was these
men who had the highest risk of developing heart disease. The "high-

I remember blowing up at my family the night before Father's Day. What a tirade! I just went on and on with my anger until I went to bed exhausted. The next morning, I felt terribly ashamed, so ashamed that I asked Catherine not to celebrate Father's Day. I didn't deserve it! I spent the day avoiding my wonderful children. I just couldn't face them.

anger" men were almost three times more likely to have a heart attack or develop angina during the follow-up period than the "low-anger" men, even after other possible influences were taken into account, such as smoking, blood pressure, cholesterol, weight, alcohol, and family history of cardiac disease. According to Dr. Kawachi, the survival of these men was largely a function of how angry they were. My own experience, based on a community survey of anger and health practices, has shown this same dose-response link between how much anger people report and their overall health risk. Those who reported higher levels of anger, my colleagues and I found, were likely to smoke more, consume more alcohol, exercise less, be more overweight, work more hours, and attend religious services less often than those reporting less anger. It is that 20 percent of the population that suffers from TAS that has the most to worry about!

EXERCISE

HOW WOULD YOU CHARACTERIZE YOUR ANGER?

1. How would you define toxic anger?
2. Are you emotionally liberated or are you just pretending? How does your

anger express itself? Make a list of the physical, emotional, and behavioral consequences of your anger.

3. What type of anger are you most likely to express: malevolent, constructive, or fractious? Do you feel more "righteous" about your anger if it is constructive? How do you think the person on the receiving end of your constructive anger feels?

CHAPTER 3

SELF-ASSESSMENT OF TOXIC ANGER

To find out if you or someone you know suffers from toxic anger, it is not necessary for you to seek the services of a mental health professional or complete a large battery of standardized psychological tests. Simply answer the following three questions as honestly and accurately as you can.* Be sure to check only one answer for each question.

TAKING THE TA TEST

1. How often during the last week did you become angry?

_____ not at all

_____ 1 or 2 times during the week

_____ 3 to 5 times during the week

_____ about 2 times each day

_____ about 3 times each day

_____ about 4 to 5 times each day

_____ about 6 to 10 times each day

_____ more than 10 times each day

* These questions are adapted from a questionnaire used by Dr. James Averill in his intensive study of anger in residents of Greenfield, Massachusetts (population 18,000), and the students at the nearby University of Massachusetts.[1]

2. On average, how intense is your anger when you get mad?

1 : 2 : 3 : 4 : 5 : 6 : 7 : 8 : 9 : 10
vory   very intense
mild   as angry as most
                                        people ever become

3. How long does your anger typically last?

_____   less than 5 minutes

_____   5 to 10 minutes

_____   less than ½ hour

_____   less than 1 hour

_____   1 to 2 hours

_____   ½ day

_____   1 day

_____   more than 1 day

SCORING THE TA TEST

HOW OFTEN DO YOU GET ANGRY?

If you checked "not at all," you are *well below average* in experiencing anger (lowest 16 percent of the reference group). If you checked "1 or 2 times a week," you are about *average* (between 17 and 82 percent). If you checked "3 to 5 times a week," you are *above average* (between 83 and 94 percent). And if you checked one of the categories indicating more than once a day, you are *well above average* (top 6 percent) when it comes to experiencing anger.

For "3 to 5 times during the week" or higher, give yourself a score of 2. Otherwise give yourself a score of 1.

> Today, I rarely get angry, my anger is never above a level 4, and it's over in five minutes or less. My TA summary score would be 1. But before I took responsibility for my anger and used the principles outlined in this book, I was angry many times a day, my anger always reached level 10, and it seemed to last forever. I was a definite 8!

HOW INTENSE IS YOUR ANGER?

If you circled 5 or below on the intensity scale, you are *below average* in terms of the strength of your anger (lowest 21 percent of the reference group). If you circled 6 or 7 on the scale, you are *average*. If you circled 8 or above, you are *above average*.

If you are in the last group (8 or above), give yourself a score of 2. Otherwise, give yourself a score of 1.

HOW LONG DOES YOUR ANGER LAST?

If you checked "less than 5 minutes" or "5 to 10 minutes," you are *below average* (29 percent of the reference group). If you checked anywhere from "less than ½ hour to 1 to 2 hours," you are *average* (between 30 and 65 percent). If you checked "½ day" or a "day," you are *above average* (between 66 and 79 percent). And if you checked "more than 1 day," you are *well above average* (top 21 percent) in the duration of your anger.

If you are in the last group ("more than 1 day"), give yourself a score of 2. Otherwise, give yourself a score of 1.

COMPUTING YOUR TA SUMMARY SCORE

By combining your three TA scores (frequency, intensity, duration), you can summarize your overall anger experience and decide at what level you (or the person you're describing) suffer from TAS. Take each score you obtained (1 or 2) and enter it into the following equation:

$$\underline{\hspace{2cm}} \times \underline{\hspace{2cm}} \times \underline{\hspace{2cm}} = \underline{\hspace{2cm}}$$

Frequency   Intensity   Duration   Summary Score

If your summary score is 1, *you do not suffer from toxic anger.* Congratulations! Your anger is like that of my friends Carla and Tom.

If your summary score is 2, *you suffer from mild TAS.* Your anger is toxic either because you get angry too often, experience anger that is too intense, or stay angry too long. Because you score high in only one area of your anger experience, you may decide that you don't really have a problem. But you do! Remember Jeffrey from Chapter 2? He fits this category; he is what I call the *occasional hothead.* Remember what his momentary flare-up of anger cost him in surgical bills? What about Peter, the man who severely hurt his infant daughter in a rare moment of rage? He fits this category too. He didn't habitually hurt his children, but he demonstrated the capacity to severely injure them *at any given moment* of frustration or provocation. For that reason alone, he was judged to be an unsafe parent.

If your summary score is 4, *you suffer from moderate TAS.* There is no question that you have problems with anger. You definitely fit into one of three categories: (1) the high-frequency/high-intensity, or *volatile* (as in volcano), category; (2) the high-frequency/long-duration, or *steamed* (as in slow-cooking vegetables), category; or (3) the high-intensity/long-duration, or *sleeping lion* (as in "don't wake up the . . ."), category. Remember John from Chapter 1, my father, or the man in the thousand-dollar suit who repeatedly abused his wife? All of them fit the volatile profile. Their anger struck often and was so intense that it led to disastrous consequences. The fact that it didn't last long was hardly a consolation!

Charles, the sixty-year-old man who kept breaking his teeth in his sleep, is an example of someone who is steamed throughout the day, only to suffer the consequences at night. Charles experiences the proverbial "slow burn." If he were more expressive about his low-intensity anger, he would, no doubt, be viewed as a chronically hostile man with a "chip on his shoulder"—more like Dennis, for example, whose anger leaked out throughout the day in sarcastic, aggressive remarks. The "slow-cooked" type of anger is most often linked to psychosomatic illnesses—hives, ulcers, colitis, hypertension, and migraine headaches—and typifies the so-called Type A, or coronary-prone, personality.

Who can you think of that fits the *sleeping lion* category, someone who rarely gets angry but when he does it is intense and lasts a long time?

If your summary score is 8, *you suffer from extreme TAS*. There is no question that anger rules your life and ruins your health and your relationships. It also affects everyone around you and spills over into their lives—your spouse, children, grandchildren, employees, coworkers, friends, neighbors—causing irrevocable harm. In his book *What You Can Change and What You Can't*, Dr. Martin Seligman notes the long-term effects of parental anger on children:

> We have followed the lives of some 400 children for the last five years, focusing on children whose parents fight (20 percent) and those whose parents divorce or separate (15 percent). We watched these 140 children carefully and contrasted them to the rest of the children. . . .
>
> The children of fighting families look the same—that is, just as bad—as the children of divorce. These children are more depressed than the children from intact families whose parents don't fight. We had hoped the difference would diminish over time, but it didn't. Three years later, these children were still more depressed than the rest of the children.
>
> Once their parents start fighting, these children become unbridled pessimists. They see bad events as permanent and pervasive, and they see themselves as responsible. Years later this pessimism persists, even after they tell us their parents are no longer fighting. Their world view has changed from the rosy optimism of childhood to the grim pessimism of a depressed adult.

My parents were not bad people. They were not uncaring or unattached from us as children. On the contrary, they saw that our clothes were clean, that we ate well, that we went to the doctor when we were ill, that we attended church regularly, that we did our homework, and that we did things together as a family. But they were intensely passionate people—both of them—and their capacity for anger seemed endless. Their anger could be ignited easily and without warning, at any time, in any circumstance, with little or no provocation. I remember many nights as a child listening to them fight and hoping that nothing bad would happen to them or us. As a result, I've spent much of my life being insecure and afraid, always afraid that something bad would happen to me or those I love.

I believe that many children react to their parents' fighting by developing a loss of security so shattering that it marks the beginning of a lifetime of dysphoria.[2]

Remember Reuben, the man whose parents didn't speak to one another for long periods after their many disagreements? Now you understand why he was depressed for "no apparent reason" during his middle years. Brian, Rachel, David, Dennis, and Aaron all suffer from extreme TAS.

SEEKING VERIFICATION

None of us is totally objective. We all have a tendency to want to see ourselves in a favorable light, especially when it comes to negative traits such as anger. We also may simply forget how many times we get mad in a week, how strong these feelings are, or how long the anger lasts. Our anger assessment may be "right on" or it may be "way off track."

To verify your TA test score, ask someone who knows you well, who interacts with you on a fairly regular basis, and whose opinion you trust to answer the self-assessment questions on the basis of their observations of you. Then compare their view of your anger with your own. If the two assessments are similar, you have a clear picture of your anger. But if your assessment is radically different from the other person's, you need to reevaluate your anger. Most often, another person's TA score for your anger will indicate a higher level than you came up with and *will be a more accurate gauge of how much you suffer from TAS*. A word of caution: Make sure the person you ask to rate your anger is not afraid of your reaction if he or she "tells it like it is."

When I asked John's (the ex-Marine) wife about his anger, her assessment coincided with his own. "He has a very short fuse, and to be honest it is hell. . . . He screams and hollers, rants and rages and cusses and carries on. . . . Just anything will set him off. . . . He'll just as soon cuss you out as look at you. . . . It is rough! . . . He'll just go on and on and on and on."

David, the angry man who had been in pain for over twenty years, and his daughter agreed on the intensity but disagreed on the frequency of his anger. He felt he got angry only "every week or two," whereas she claimed he got angry "more than once a week." When I showed him her assessment compared with his own, he was genuinely shocked and distressed.

Another way to verify the accuracy of your TA scores is to keep an anger diary for a week. In a notebook, keep track of each time you get annoyed or angry, every day, in each instance noting the following:

- ♦ Date
- ♦ Time of day
- ♦ Whether you were annoyed or angry
- ♦ How intense your feeling of annoyance or anger was on a 10-point scale
- ♦ How long the feeling lasted

After a week, your anger diary might look like this:

Date	Time	Annoyed/Angry	Intensity	Duration
11/16/95	9:15 A.M.	angry	5	10 min.
	4:23 P.M.	annoyed	3	2 min.
11/17/95	10:45 A.M.	angry	7	30 min.
11/18/95	—	—	—	—
11/19/95	11:26 A.M.	angry	8	60 min.
	2:15 P.M.	angry	7	30 min.
	4:35 P.M.	annoyed	5	5 min.
	9:30 P.M.	angry	6	20 min.
11/20/95	11:02 A.M.	annoyed	3	3 min.
11/21/95	—	—	—	—
11/22/95	5:15 P.M.	angry	4	20 min.

Over a week's time, this person got angry about once a day, had an intensity score of approximately 6, and typically remained angry for less than one-half hour.

These two assessment methods are fairly comparable for assessing the *intensity* and *duration* of one's anger. However, Dr. Averill found that the average answer to the frequency-of-anger question on the questionnaire was "one to two times during the week," whereas it was "about one time each day" when subjects used diaries. The frequency varies because we are more likely to remember only those episodes of anger that are especially intense or that last a long time, and thus we risk *underestimating* our potential for TA.

Because it is important to have the truest possible anger profile as you begin to read this book, I suggest you do all the following: (1) take the TA test, (2) get a second opinion, and (3) keep the anger diary for a week.

HOW DIS-GUISED IS YOUR ANGER?

In his excellent book *Anger: How to Recognize and Cope with It,* Dr. Leo Madow points out that "our language is replete with masked expressions for anger, ranging from pleasant-sounding but clearly substitute phrases to complete denial of anger."[3] Few of us come right out and say, "I'm really angry about what you just did!" Instead, we are more likely to water down or *dis*-guise our angry feelings by saying how *dis*-appointed, *dis*-gusted, or *dis*-pleased we are with someone else's behavior.

For example, a few years ago the parents of an adolescent came to me about their son's pattern of academic underachievement and acting-out behavior, which was a huge source of frustration for them. When I asked how they felt about their son's troublesome behavior, they only said, "Well, of course, we're disappointed in him." When I asked these nice people if that was the best they could come up with, the father rather quietly responded, "I guess. How would you feel?" I then said, "Well, I'd probably be angry as hell and might feel like wringing his neck!" At which point, the young man jumped up and said to his parents, "Let's get out of here; this man's crazy!" And the father replied—with a hint of irritation in his voice—"You go if you want. Your mother and I want to hear what the doctor's got to say." These parents were simply unaware of their own anger toward their son, and as a result they were unable to set effective limits on his outrageous behavior.

Anger is usually disguised, according to Dr. Madow, when the individual perceives it as overwhelming. *The very people who are carrying around the most anger may, ironically, be the least aware of it.* "Disguised" anger, trapped in the body, can result in physical disease such as hypertension, clogged arteries, strokes, and depression, as demonstrated in the cases of Charles and Dennis.

How *dis*-guised is your anger? Start listening to yourself. Pay particular attention to how often you say you are feeling any of the following:

Dis-agreeable	Dis-appointed	Dis-enchanted
Dis-gusted	Dis-heartened	Dis-interested
Dis-illusioned	Dis-mal	Dis-mayed
Dis-pleased	Dis-tant	Dis-tracted
Dis-stressed	Dis-concerted	Dis-connected
Dis-contented	Dis-couraged	Dis-dainful
Dis-gruntled	Dis-liked	Dis-respectful
Dis-traught	Dis-turbed	Dis-trustful

The feeling underlying all of these feelings may be anger.

♦ ♦ ♦

By now, you've no doubt decided that you (or someone you know) suffers from TAS. Good for you. *All behavioral change begins with awareness.* This is the first step toward freeing yourself from toxic anger once and for all.

CHAPTER 4

THE ANGRY DISPOSITION
A Psychobiological Perspective

Anger is never without a reason,
but seldom a good one.
—Benjamin Franklin,
Poor Richard's Almanac

Anger is an emotion, and thus, by definition, it is beyond our conscious reason, at least in the moment we experience it. Emotions have traditionally been considered reflexive or involuntary experiences rather than willful acts. We do not simply "choose" to be angry, happy, or sad; rather, emotions choose us. Likewise, emotions are feelings, so they reflect a change in both our biological and our psychological state. When we become angry, we are both mentally and physically stimulated. The "mental" component of anger or any other emotion involves a psychological matrix of thoughts, beliefs, expectations, and values that make each of us a unique personality. The "physical" component directly relates to a change in our biological state—increased heart rate, blood pressure, skin temperature—which differs in intensity and volatility from one person to the next.

BIOLOGICAL AROUSAL

Biologically, anger is defined as a stress response of the human nervous system to internal or external demands, threats, and pressures. When we are faced with a threat to our survival, our nervous system instantly and automatically prepares us to meet that threat by raising our defenses. This is true whether we are faced with critical life events that force us to change or with the minor irritants that punctuate everyday life. Our nervous system does not wait for a conscious interpretation of the events in question; *it just reacts!*

This built-in defense mechanism is found in the sympathetic branch of our autonomic nervous system, which is primarily responsible for expending physical energy and "calling us to arms." The defense response is triggered by the release of the hormone adrenaline, secreted by the adrenal gland, which is attached to the kidney. Adrenaline causes pupil dilatation, rapid heartbeat, rising blood pressure, and rapid breathing. The liver responds by releasing sugar, and blood shifts from internal organs to skeletal muscles, causing a general state of tension. *At this point, we are aroused and ready to react to whatever comes next!*

Dr. Hans Selye, the preeminent stress researcher of the twentieth century, saw this biological "alarm reaction" as the first stage of a general adaptation syndrome (GAS).[1] The GAS, according to Selye, is the body's way of dealing with all types of stressors, from a bacterial infection to an unexpected visit by a neighbor. Dr. Walter B. Cannon, a noted Harvard physiologist, forty years earlier had referred to this pattern of biological arousal as the *fight-or-flight response*, an involuntary mechanism shared with all other species of animals.[2]

Dr. Selye particularly emphasized the nonspecific nature of this alarm reaction in humans. He said the same basic reaction occurs whether you receive good or bad news and regardless of which emotion you feel: fear, excitement, surprise, or anger. The difference in the reaction is found not in the biology of the emotion but in the psychological mind-set that accompanies it.

PSYCHOLOGICAL AROUSAL

From a psychological perspective, two factors make anger unique. First, *anger is a response to a perceived misdeed,* usually on the part of others. You feel angry because you believe that you have been wronged. Second, and more important, *anger involves an attribution of blame* in connection with that perceived misdeed. You target someone or something as the cause of your anger. Both conditions must be met in order to experience anger. You may feel tense or anxious if you are biologically but not psychologically aroused by a particular situation or encounter, but you are not likely to experience anger.

It is important to understand that anger is a reaction to your perception of how other people treat you as well as your judgment of their actions. Was their response arbitrary ("He didn't have to do that, but he did!") or intentional ("She did that on purpose!")? If you don't feel slighted or mistreated, you will not become angry. Whether or not you were, in fact, mistreated is irrelevant. How you perceive your treatment dictates your anger response. Similarly, if you feel mistreated, but think that it was unavoidable ("It was an accident") or unintentional ("She really didn't mean to do it"), you will not get angry. The fact that the other person may have intended to mistreat you, again, makes no difference. Only your perception counts! *Anger, like beauty, is always in the eye of you, the beholder.*

Remember the two customers in the restaurant, one of whom was clearly angry ("What do I have to do to get some service around here!") and the other not ("Actually, I wanted the steak well done")? The behavior of the waitress had nothing to do with how each of these men felt. On the contrary, their feelings were the result of how each man *perceived* the waitress's behavior. Customer A felt mistreated by the waitress and blamed her. He believed she was capable of providing him better service "if she wanted to." Customer B fortunately saw the spilled food for what it was—an accident. The waitress did not purposely spill the food on him, so she was not to blame and he felt no anger.

> My life hasn't changed much in recent years. People still cut in front of me when I'm driving, the guy ahead of me in the express line has too many items, I leave phone messages and no one calls back. The difference is my response to life. I no longer expect things always to go my way or become angry when they don't. I realize that I have no more right to the "good life" than anyone else. Once I understood this simple principle, my life became much less of a struggle.

TRIGGERING EVENTS AND CIRCUMSTANCES

If you ask people what makes them angry, they invariably describe an event or circumstance that falls into one or more of the following four categories:

1. You become angry when someone demeans you or attacks your self-esteem; this category includes physical as well as verbal abuse.

   > I was talking to my supervisor about our Christmas bonus and he asked, "Why do you think you deserve one?" The anger hit me and I could feel the heat going to my face. It made me actually sick. I was so mad, you know?
   > —Maryanne, age forty-one

2. You become angry when someone or something prevents you from reaching a significant goal that you believe is rightfully yours. You are less likely to become angry if you are not strongly committed to the goal or you do not feel entitled to reach the goal.

   > Joe came to see me as soon as he heard I had been offered the manager's job. I could see he was really angry. We had been the best of friends for years, but that didn't seem to matter now. He

asked me not to accept the offer if I wanted to remain friends. He felt the job was rightfully his. He'd been with the company longer and until a year ago had been my supervisor. I understood how he felt, honestly I did, but I couldn't turn down the job. He never spoke to me after that except in the normal course of business—no more golf, no more beer after work.

—Stephen, age thirty-eight

3. You typically become angry when someone or something violates your basic principles or values, such as fair play, honesty, equity, and responsibility in human relationships. The more strongly committed you are to certain principles and values, the more likely you are to get angry.

I've never seen my wife, Miriam, that angry in all the years we've been married. She got all over that woman who was hitting her child there in the department store. The woman yelled at her, even threatened her, but she stood her ground. Miriam just couldn't stand by and watch anyone abuse a child. I was really proud of her.

—Phillip, age thirty-two

4. You become angry when you feel helpless to correct a "wrong" or to fix a situation that has gone awry.

I have three small kids. . . . The other day, I went to get something out of the freezer we have in the carport. Everything was spoiled—six hundred dollars' worth of meat we had just bought, all gone! The kids must have knocked the plug out of the wall while they were playing. I got so mad that my wife took the kids down to her parents. I guess she was afraid I would do something crazy. I just felt so helpless standing there looking at all that ruined meat!

—Carl, age twenty-eight

To better understand how easily your anger is psychologically triggered, read the following list of potentially upsetting situations and indicate how you would feel after each one:*

0   =   I would not feel angry or annoyed.
1   =   I would feel annoyed, but not angry.
2   =   I would feel a little angry.
3   =   I would feel somewhat angry.
4   =   I would feel very angry.

_____ 1. You unpack an appliance you have just bought, plug it in, and discover that it doesn't work.
_____ 2. You are overcharged by a repairperson.
_____ 3. Your car gets stuck in the mud or snow.
_____ 4. You are talking to someone who does not answer you.
_____ 5. Someone you know pretends to be something he is not.
_____ 6. While you are struggling to carry four cups of coffee to your table at a cafeteria, someone bumps into you, and the coffee spills.
_____ 7. You are the butt of a joke or someone teases you.
_____ 8. You accidently make a wrong turn in a parking lot. As you get out of your car, someone yells at you, "Where did you learn to drive?"
_____ 9. You are blamed for someone else's mistakes.

*Adapted from an anger scale developed by Dr. Raymond Novaco at the University of California, Irvine. The full scale contains eighty items.[3]

_____ 10. You try to concentrate, but a person near you is tapping her foot.

_____ 11. You lend someone an important book or tool, and she fails to return it.

_____ 12. You have had a busy day, and the person you live with starts to complain to you about something that you forgot to do.

_____ 13. You are engaged in a discussion with someone who persists in arguing about a topic he knows very little about.

_____ 14. You need to get somewhere quickly, but the car in front of you is going 25 mph in a 40-mph zone and you can't pass.

_____ 15. Hurrying to get somewhere, you tear a good pair of slacks on a sharp object.

_____ 16. Using your last quarter to make a phone call, you are disconnected before you finish dialing and the quarter is lost.

Add up your numbers to determine your level of *psychological arousal* (PA): _____

Your PA score indicates how likely you are to get angry on a day-to-day basis because of your thoughts, beliefs, and convictions. If your PA score is between 0 and 32, you are less anger prone than the average person. If you scored between 33 and 43, your tendency to become angry is about average. If your PA score is between 44 and 50, your anger is triggered more easily than the average person. And if you scored 51 or above, you have a hair-trigger temper! People who suffer from toxic anger (TAS) definitely fall into the last two categories.

INTUITIVE ANGER

At this point, you may be confused by my definitions of anger. First, I demonstrated that emotions like anger are by their very nature irrational and thus beyond conscious reason. Then, I suggested that anger is the result of each person's perception of particular situations in everyday life. How is it possible that anger can be part of our thinking at the same time that it is beyond our reason? This seeming contradiction can be explained with reference to intuition.

Intuition is the process by which our mind knows something to be true without our conscious reasoning. It is the "early-warning system" that humans possess that enables us to react instantly to situations that may potentially benefit or harm us. Intuition is the "hunch" that tells us how other people will treat us. It is our "sixth sense."

Neuroscientist Antoine Bechara at the University of Iowa College of Medicine studied the vital role that intuition plays in human adaptation.[4] He and his fellow researchers performed an experiment in which both normal and brain-damaged subjects tried to win money by gambling with different decks of cards. The decks were rigged to be either "advantageous," allowing the players to win money, or "disadvantageous," causing the players to lose money. After a few losses, the non-brain-damaged subjects demonstrated a rise in their skin temperature when playing with the bad decks and began to avoid them. When these subjects were interrupted early in the game and asked what they thought was going on, they reported that they "did not have a clue." When they were interrupted later, however, some had a "hunch" that they were more likely to win with certain decks than others. In contrast, the brain-damaged subjects "failed to generate autonomic (emotional) responses and continued to select cards from the bad decks." In effect, they lacked the capacity for intuition. They had suffered damage to the ventromedial prefrontal cortex, which is the part of the brain that stores *dispositional knowledge* from the past. It is in this region of the brain, according to Dr. Bechara, that a lifetime of accumulated mental "records shaped by reward, punishment, and the emotions that attend them" are kept at our disposal to be used in dealing with today's problems, challenges, and conflicts. Anger is clearly one type of "attending emotion" that results from this

I instantly disliked Walter. He was a bully and demanded that we do everything his way. He took all the fun out of our annual trek down the James River. I spent three days in angry silence, hiding in my tent and sulking, before I realized why Walter had such a negative effect on me. He reminded me so much of my father—his physical build, the sound of his voice, and his aggressive behavior. No wonder everything he said or did made me angry.

intuitive process. Thus, we find ourselves becoming angry in situations today that remind our (unconscious) brain of similar situations from our past in which we also were angry and in which anger served some useful purpose. Anger—without any effort on our part—thus becomes self-perpetuating.

Intuition can give us an advantage in our present-day surroundings—help us be winners rather than losers. But does it always? In the case of toxic anger, it may be a decided disadvantage, triggering anger in situations in which it is neither appropriate nor helpful. *What worked for us at some earlier point in time now works against us!*

THE ROLE OF TEMPERAMENT

There is no such thing as an angry temperament. However, certain temperamental qualities determine whether a person will experience normal or toxic anger. Temperament is a set of inherited traits that define the *style* of our emotional and behavioral responses—the *tone* and *direction* of our emotions. Dr. Avshalom Caspi of Harvard University, for example, distinguishes among the angry, ill-tempered person who moves against the world; the shy person who moves away from the world; and the dependent person who moves toward the world.[5]

Dr. Arnold Buss, a psychologist at the University of Texas, identifies the person most likely to become angry or act aggressively with reference to the following four temperamental characteristics:[6]

- ♦ Impulsivity
- ♦ High activity
- ♦ Behavioral and physiological hyperreactivity
- ♦ Independence

The highly *impulsive* person cannot delay gratification or tolerate the frustration that ensues when his or her needs are not quickly and easily met. When confronted with a potentially anger-arousing situation, the impulsive person must act immediately and decisively by getting angry. The *highly active* person expends more energy than the average person in the course of a day and is much more likely to have interactions with people that provoke anger. The *hyperreactive* individual responds in a more intense and vigorous manner than most people. As Brian put it, "Where another person gets a little upset, I'm angry!" Last, the *independent* individual chafes and becomes angry more often in response to strong interpersonal pressures to conform and submit to societal demands and restrictions.

Impulsivity, activity level, and independence define the frequency with which we become angry, whereas reactivity defines the intensity and duration of our anger.

How does your temperament define your anger? Circle the one number on each of the following dimensions of temperament that best describes you:

+2	+1	−1	−2
Impulsive/quick to act			Deliberate/thoughtful

+2	+1	−1	−2
Active/energetic			Passive/nonenergetic

+2	+1	−1	−2
Intense/excitable			Calm/placid

+2	+1	−1	−2
Independent/self-reliant			Dependent/rely on others

Add up your numbers to determine your *biological arousal* (BA) score: _____

If you have a negative BA score, anger should not to be a problem for you. If your BA score is positive, however, you probably get angry too often, feel anger too intensely, or stay angry too long. In short, you suffer from TAS.*

TEMPERAMENTAL CONTINUITY

Temperament is defined in early childhood and doesn't drastically change over a lifetime. If you were a happy five-year-old, you can expect to be a reasonably happy eighty-five-year-old. Similarly, if you were an ill-tempered, easily upset child, you will be the same irascible individual throughout your life unless, of course, you make a concerted effort to change.

Continuity of temperament exists for two primary reasons.[7] One, *we tend to seek environments—people and situations—that are compatible with our temperament.* We look for a situation in which our style will "work." A socially extroverted individual may seek a job in marketing because it offers him more day-to-day variation in work demands and more of a challenge, whereas an introverted person may prefer working as a laboratory technician or computer operator because the job requirements are more routine and involve less contact with people.

Second, *we tend to act in ways that consistently provoke the same coun-*

*Preliminary research findings from my laboratory suggest that impulsivity and hyperreactivity may be more strongly linked to the development of TAS than the other two traits.

> My father was an intelligent man who worked at blue-collar jobs most of his life. I remember once they made him a salesman, and for a time he wore a shirt and tie to work every day and he had to be nice to people. He made more money, but he hated it. He liked jobs where he could get angry during the day, yell at people, and they would yell back. . . . That's where he fit, where he seemed to be happy.

terreactions in others, which then reinforce or sustain our temperamental style. Anger begets anger. Love begets love. John, the sixty-year-old ex-Marine, for example, began his cycle of anger during his early school years. He was treated as an outsider by the other children, so he fought back by being angry and aggressive. But this behavior only made him more of an outsider, and in turn, he became even more angry and aggressive. Fifty years later, he still feels like an outsider, even from his family, and he is still ready to fight.

PUTTING THE PIECES TOGETHER: A CONCEPTUAL MODEL FOR TOXIC ANGER

Toxic anger results from a combination of biological and psychological response patterns that distinguish TAS from lesser forms of anger and other emotional experiences such as fear, pleasure, and depression. We are disposed to toxic anger because of a combustible interaction of temperament ("moving against the world") and a learned worldview. *If* the world treats you unfairly, *if* the world interrupts your goal-seeking behavior, and *if* you experience a transitional or chronic state of generalized (biological) distress too often, then you most assuredly will suffer from toxic anger.

No one begins life experiencing toxic anger. Temperament may give us a boost toward TAS, but the rest of our behavior is learned. Anger "fixes" certain life situations, if only for the moment. The baby screams angrily, and her mother comes running to feed and comfort her. The child throws an angry tantrum in the grocery store, and his mother buys him the candy she had said he could not have. The customer yells, "My coffee's cold, I want some hot coffee!" and gets more coffee. Thus, we learn intuitively that anger gives us a decided advantage in day-to-day interactions. Quite naturally, we repeat behavior that works and may even seek out circumstances—marriage, job, friends—suited to our ill-tempered disposition. Anger becomes, in effect, one of the primary "attending emotions" that shape our lives. All too quickly, anger becomes an overlearned, overgeneralized response to life stress. The screaming baby, the tempestuous child, and the outraged adult all represent different developmental stages of an emerging TAS.

♦ ♦ ♦

You may now be aware that life has set you on a course of toxic anger. Unless this course is altered, the anger not only will follow you throughout your life, but it may also drive you to an early grave. Fortunately, you can easily alter your lifestyle (and thus life course) to avoid the inevitable costs and consequences of toxic anger.

EXERCISE

WHY ARE YOU SO ANGRY?

1. Ask a parent or someone who knew you as a child what you were like. Have that person rate you on the temperament scale that you completed in this chapter. How close is that score to the score you came up with?
2. Give the "psychological arousal" test to someone you know who appears to see life differently than you do. Is his or her PA score different from your own? Discuss the situations in which the two of you responded very differently. Try to "see the world" through this person's eyes.

3. Make a list of experiences from your past that may have shaped your disposition both toward (+) and away from (−) toxic anger. Are there more pluses than minuses?

4. The next time you find yourself getting angry, check with someone else to see if your "intuition" about being mistreated is valid. You may find that you can't always trust your intuition.

CHAPTER 5

REDEFINING THE PROBLEM

We have met the enemy,
and he is us.

—Pogo (cartoon character)

Most people fail to eliminate toxic anger from their daily lives in large part because they are trying to change how other people treat them instead of changing their own behavior.

IT IS TIME TO INTERNALIZE

When I ask people why they are angry, they tell me things like: "Those people at the paint store, they wouldn't do what they said they would do. They promised to do the work and they didn't." "They canceled my cable television just because I forgot to pay the bill one month. And they were so hateful about it." "Everything I do at work, someone checks to see if I did it right. I'm the most competent person there, and they want to make sure I do my job right."

These people all externalize their anger. Like most of us, they see the cause of their anger as outside of themselves. Their focus is on "those people," "they," and "someone" rather than their own emotional response. If only "they" would change—do the job they were supposed to

Toxic Anger Checklist

At this point, I do not expect you to understand fully why you suffer from TAS. That will become clearer as you read Chapters 8 through 17. After you complete each chapter, indicate on this checklist whether the factor discussed in that chapter plays a role in *your* toxic anger:

_____ Personality: narcissistic, cynical, catastrophic, compulsive

_____ Stress

_____ Passivity

_____ Substance use

_____ Lack of empathy

_____ Excess tension buildup or energy deficit

_____ Depression

_____ Maladaptive coping

_____ Failure to communicate

_____ Codependency

do, not cancel my TV, quit checking up on me—then I would be free of these angry feelings. Right? Wrong!

As I have already discussed, *the cause of anger lies not in the actions of others but in our own unique biological and psychological reactivity.* We should be asking ourselves why we get angry at what others are doing instead of what others are doing that makes us angry.

♦ ♦ ♦

For the past thirty years, I have worked with people suffering from chronic musculoskeletal pain and often listen to the frustrations of the physicians who are unable to make their pain disappear. Recently, one of these physicians asked for my help with a pain patient. "I just dread seeing that woman's name on the list," he said. "It's always the same thing—she comes in crying, complaining of pain, and asking what I'm going to do about it. I've tried everything I know over the past two years, but none of it seems to ease the pain. I don't know what else to do."

The advice I gave him was this: "When she comes in the next time, why don't you turn things around and ask her what she intends to do about her pain? Is she, for example, willing to lose some weight? Maybe quite smoking? Learn meditation? Or what about volunteer work as a distraction from the endless pain? Put the responsibility on her. It's her pain after all."

My physician friend stood there for a minute with a look of utter disbelief on his face and said, "Doyle, I can't do that! This poor woman's coming to me for help. I have to do something for her. I just don't know what. I can't ask her to fix her own pain." He was clearly not pleased with my advice.

"In that case," I said, "nothing is going to change. The two of you will dance that same old dance forever even though you both obviously hate the tune."

♦ ♦ ♦

And so it is with anger. What would you think if I said to you, "Forget how others are treating you. Focus on what is happening inside of you—*your* thoughts, *your* temperament, *your* level of autonomic arousal. Make it your anger, not theirs!" You would most likely experience the same initial sense of disbelief and disappointment as that physician did. Because he externalized the woman's pain and made it his own problem, he was failing miserably at making her pain go away. This is exactly what angry people tend to do with anger: *We try to make it someone else's problem.* We direct all our energy into coercing others to change "their" behavior, which is a frustrating and fruitless task that only makes us angrier.

HOW AROUSABLE ARE YOU?

Anger is clearly linked to *arousability*. As I demonstrated in the preceding chapter, anger arousal involves a complex of psychological and biological factors that combine to bring us to the point of anger. Temperament is no more important than intuition; generalized distress is no less important than how we perceive and interpret the actions of others. All these factors play a role in escalating our anger and must be dealt with if we are to free ourselves from toxic anger.

◆ ◆ ◆

Remember John, the sixty-year-old machinist who was too arousable? When I first met him, his PA score was 54, which put him in the highest category of psychological arousal, and his BA score was +7, suggesting an equally high level of biological arousal. John definitely suffered from TAS.

Carla (mentioned in Chapter 2), on the other hand, had a different "arousability" profile. Her PA score was 20, which placed her in the lowest level of psychological arousal, and her BA score was +1. Carla rarely got angry.

John and Carla are both energetic and self-reliant; however, they have drastically different levels of arousal. John is impulsive and excitable, whereas Carla tends to be thoughtful and calm. They have distinctly different worldviews. John has a fixed notion about how life *should* be: "If you pay good money for something, it *should* work. People *should* keep their mouths shut if they don't know what they're talking about." He gets angry when life does not conform to his expectations. Carla, on the other hand, doesn't expect people to conform to her worldview. Although she clearly acknowledges that many people are "disrespectful and unkind," she does not insist that they adopt her standards of civil and ethical conduct.

◆ ◆ ◆

Where do you fall on the continuum of anger arousability? Were you below average, average, or above average for psychological arousal and biological arousal? Using the grid on the next page, fill in your PA and BA scores to calculate your potential for TAS.

PA Score

	0 to 32	33 to 43	44 to 64
−2 to −8	LOW	LOW	MOD
−1 to +3	LOW	MOD	HIGH
+4 to +8	MOD	HIGH	HIGH

BA Score

This grid will also help you decide which of the TA "solution" chapters are most suited to your needs. If, for example, you are high on psychological arousal (low BA, high PA) only, you will want to pay particular attention to chapters dealing with the following:

- Toxic personality traits
- Assertive relationships
- Empathy
- Coping strategies
- Communication
- Codependency

On the other hand, if you score high only on biological arousal (high BA, low PA), you will be more interested in chapters dealing with these issues:

- Stress
- Substance use
- Exercise
- Depression

However, if you, like many others, score high on both biological and psychological arousal, you will want to read the entire book!

AROUSABILITY IS NOT A CONSTANT

Emotional arousability is not a constant. It can change throughout our lives. Sometimes we can deal with life's many complexities and challenges and feel nothing more than occasional annoyance; at other times, we respond to the very same challenges like a "raging bull." Changes in arousability can be gradual or abrupt, and they leave us more or less prone to toxic anger, as illustrated by the case of Marie. Marie is a forty-nine-year-old divorcée whose peaceful temperament is obvious to anyone who is around her for more than a minute. Marie laughs continuously; everyone who knows her likes her; and, most important, she likes herself. Her BA score now is +1, and her PA score is 31. She has a low potential for anger arousal.

But Marie was not always at peace with herself. In fact, until six years ago (shortly after she became divorced), she was quite the opposite. Marie was angry all the time and had been ever since she was a child. As a youngster, she would bite other kids who made her mad or tell lies to get them into trouble. "One time," she said, "I was really mad with this boy, so I pulled a loose thread on my skirt until it all unraveled and then ran and told the teacher that he tore it." She added, "And he got punished." As an adult, she once got angry enough to try to hit a woman with her car. "I would let the air out of people's tires, pitch a knife right past my husband's head, break dishes on the sidewalk just to see them shatter, attempt suicide, and even call my minister a faggot."

Marie had a very unhappy childhood. She was mistreated and made to feel unwanted from the day she was born. She learned to think of herself as so "bad" that she was "only put on this earth to die." She was constantly struggling with the people around her. By her actions, she was telling them, "You can't make me move!" The death of her year-old son and a bad marriage of twenty-four years only compounded her anger.

She emphasized that "these events did not make me angry; they just made me *more* angry!" Thinking back about that time, Marie gives herself a BA score of +8 and a PA score of 58, which put her in the super-high range of anger arousal.

She is not sure exactly how or when she began to "set aside" her toxic anger. She only knows that she has changed. "One morning I woke up and discovered that I liked myself, that I wasn't really a bad person after all." From then on, she gradually began to feel and act less angry. Her whole view of the world has changed. In the past, if someone ahead of her was going 25 mph in a 40-mph zone, she would "tailgate them, put my bright lights on, and call them all kinds of bad names." Now, in the exact same situation, instead she thinks, "They're out there for a reason. They keep me from getting tickets!"

◆ ◆ ◆

Michael, a thirty-six-year-old pain client, had a similar change in anger arousability, only in the opposite direction. It has been nine years since Michael injured his back on the job, and four years since he had unsuccessful back surgery. In the years that I helped him cope more realistically with the limitations chronic pain placed on his lifestyle, I never viewed him as an angry man. He became anxious and frustrated sometimes, and even clinically depressed, but never angry.

However, Michael changed recently. I had not seen Michael for several months when he came into my office uncharacteristically tense, agitated to the point of tears, and with an angry look on his face. He was not sure himself exactly what he was feeling, but he said, "I'm not acting like myself!" It seemed that for several weeks he found himself leaving home time and again "so I wouldn't do something stupid." On one occasion that greatly disturbed him, he angrily shoved his young son against the wall because the boy was arguing with his sister. He loves his children tremendously, and he had never before touched them in anger. In our session, he talked about financial pressures that had been building up at home for some time as a result of his long-term unemployment and the fact that he could not bring himself to "sit my family down and say no" when they wanted things they could not afford. Bills were not getting paid, creditors were hounding him, and he was feeling more and more stressed each day.

Michael's BA and PA scores, until recently, had been −1 and 14, respectively (suggesting a low potential for anger arousal), but now they were +2 and 48 (suggesting a high level of anger arousability). What had changed was not his temperament but his worldview. He was suddenly looking at the world and the actions of everyone around him, including loved ones, through the eyes of someone who felt trapped and unable to control his economic destiny.

However, because anger arousability is not constant, *positive change is possible!* You do not have to live (and die) with your toxic anger. All you need to do is read Chapters 8 through 17, complete the Toxic Anger Checklist, and then decide which of the various behavioral prescriptions listed—all aimed at decreasing arousability—offer you the best chance of success.

EXERCISE

HOW AROUSED ARE YOU COMPARED TO OTHERS?

See if you can get five people you know to complete the PA and BA tests found in Chapter 4. Choose some people who get angry easily and often, as well as some who do not. Plot their scores on the "arousability" grid. Does their personal toxic anger profile match up with your own observations? How did they react when you showed them where they fell on the grid?

CHAPTER 6

WHAT'S IN IT FOR ME?

Since I took control of my anger,
I have a peaceful mind.
I don't have to go to bed every night
wondering what I have to do
to get even with someone.
—Marie

Changing behavior is not easy because behavior tends to be self-perpetuating. According to common wisdom, "the best guide to the future can be found in the past."

It is not enough to know you have a problem. Most smokers know that smoking is bad for their health, but they continue to smoke. Most obese people know that they should lose weight, yet they continue to overeat. Most alcoholics know they are destroying their liver and brain with every drink they take, but they continue to consume alcohol.

For behavioral changes to take place, two conditions must be met. First, you need to have an *intentional attitude* about changing your behavior. Second, you must have one or more *disincentives*, or reasons to stop the behavior.

When I went into therapy eight years ago, I was not looking for someone to help me with my anger. I was there because I was severely depressed. But therapy helped me understand the key role that anger played in my mood disorder. Every time I got mad, my mood would turn in a downward direction. Then I exploded in rage, and I would feel better for a while. I seemed to cycle back and forth. Learning to control anger became the cornerstone of my treatment. I started out intending to be less depressed and ended up being less angry.

INTENTIONAL ATTITUDE

Psychologists James Prochaska and Carlo DiClemente recently identified five stages of *intentional attitude,* or readiness, that a person displays when changing maladaptive behavior.[1] In the first, the stage of *no intention,* the person does not consider changing his behavior. He is happy with the status quo and has no wish to behave differently. Typically, he resists, either actively or passively, any efforts to change his mind. In the second, the stage of *preintention,* the person has identified the problem and explores the possibility of change in the near future, usually within six months. However, he is not ready to commit himself to the process of change. In the third stage, the *preparation* stage, the person develops a plan of action to begin the change process. In the fourth, the *action* stage, he takes specific steps to change his unwanted behavior. Finally, in the fifth, or *maintenance,* stage, he has succeeded in maintaining his "new" behavior for at least six months. In these final three stages, the *intentional* stages, he is not only ready for change, *he is operational!*

In which of these five stages do you find yourself when evaluating your toxic anger? If someone gave you this book (as opposed to your buying it yourself), and you wondered why he or she bought the book for you, you are definitely in the no-intention stage. Similarly, if it irritates you that someone suggests you may be "too angry for your own good," you too are in the no-intention stage. However, if you are already aware that you get angry much too often and you are beginning to think that it isn't healthy, you have at least progressed to the preintentional stage. If you purchased this book or have considered seeking professional help with this problem, you are contemplating (preintention) change. If, on the other hand, you have definitely decided to become less angry and you are hoping this book will provide you with a specific plan of action, you are in the preparation stage. You may even be in the action or main-tenance stage and simply have purchased this book to see if you can learn anything more to add to your program of freeing yourself from toxic anger. Good for you!

(Fill in the blank.) At this point, I am at the _____ stage. However, I would like to progress to the _____ stage.

♦ ♦ ♦

My wife and I recently conducted an "anger screen" at a health and safety fair in our local community. More than three hundred men and women, ranging from thirteen to eighty-three years of age, took the tests here in Chapters 3, 4, and 5 and received instant feedback about whether or not they suffered from toxic anger. Clearly, all but a handful of these people participated out of curiosity, not because they thought they had a prob-lem with anger. However, many left with a completely different attitude. In fact, more than half of them, men and women alike, appeared to ex-perience anger at a toxic level. This group's biggest problem was the frequency of their anger—three to five times a week on the average. Making people aware that they have a problem is the primary reason for conducting a health screen in the first place. To move those people who need help from one stage of intention ("There's nothing wrong with me!") to another ("Maybe I should have this checked out further?") is the chal-lenge. If reading this book does for you what the anger screening did for so many of our neighbors, then you have succeeded. *You are one step closer to change.*

FIRST THE BOOK, THEN THE THERAPY

Anger therapy, like therapy for other types of disorders, typically fails if the client is not ready for change. Cliff is a good example: A man in his late sixties, Cliff had recently retired from a thirty-year career in engineering because of serious health problems. Several months before he came to me for treatment, he suffered a heart attack followed by quadruple bypass surgery. His wife and his cardiologist both felt he needed help in controlling his anger. Cliff admitted that he came from a family in which "everyone seemed to have a temper." For most of his life, he had gotten angry repeatedly throughout the day, usually when a situation did not go his way or other people did not live up to the high standards he set for himself. His anger was always intense but was usually over quickly.

Cliff came to treatment four times. In these sessions, I learned that he had suffered many personal losses throughout his life and, from early childhood, had also suffered from chronic low self-esteem. Cliff was a classic "underdog," and anger was his only defense against what he saw as a lifetime of injustice.

Cliff failed to show up for his fifth appointment, and I never saw him again. Although I was disappointed that he did not remain in treatment long enough to benefit from the experience, I was not surprised by his early departure. He clearly displayed the wrong attitude to succeed in therapy. He was not ready for help and was there only to satisfy his wife and doctor. He did not want or intend to change.

Cliff's response to treatment is not unusual. As one leading proponent of anger therapy put it, people who need help the most "often stubbornly cling to their anger," either because they fail to recognize they have a problem or because they believe their toxic anger is justified.[2] This is especially true for angry clients whose referral is initiated by others.

DISINCENTIVES

Incentives are important when you want to begin a new behavior. They are rewards that exert a positive influence over whatever behavior they follow. Disincentives, on the other hand, are negative, or punitive, and they provide a motive to stop old, maladaptive behavior. Disincentives represent the costs we incur when we engage in a particular behavior. Some of these costs are tangible (financial, medical, legal, occupational), whereas others are intangible (social, emotional).

There are seven major disincentives for being overly angry that should be considered:

♦ Toxic anger can make you physically and mentally ill.
♦ Toxic anger can shorten your life expectancy.
♦ Toxic anger contributes to marital instability, marital conflict, and divorce.
♦ Toxic anger limits one's educational attainment and occupational status, and it contributes to occupational instability.
♦ Toxic anger reduces one's effectiveness as a parent.
♦ Toxic anger acts as a barrier to intimacy in social relationships and contributes to social alienation and loneliness.
♦ Toxic anger is economically costly.

Some of the cases I have already discussed provide examples of how toxic anger can compromise mental and physical health. John had a hiatal hernia as a result of being too angry. David had a heart attack. Dennis and Reuben were both depressed. Charles suffered from severe bruxism, Aaron mercilessly chewed up the inside of his mouth, and Jeffrey broke his hand. All jeopardized their health because of excessive anger. In his best-selling *The Angry Book,* Dr. Theodore Isaac Rubin suggests other ways in which anger "poisons" our health, including chronic anxiety, eating disorders (obesity, anorexia), sleep disorders (insomnia, hypersomnia), obsessive-compulsive behavior, phobias, and high blood pres-

> I'd like to say that I began to take control of my anger because I was concerned it was destroying my marriage or making my kids afraid of me, but it wasn't anything that noble. My sole motive was to regain my sanity. And even today, that's why I work hard to keep from getting angry—not so that I can be a better husband or father but so that I can stay sane! I know that sounds terribly selfish, but it works for me.

sure.[3] Evidence from individual medical studies has also linked high levels of expressed or unexpressed anger to illnesses such as glaucoma, hives, asthma, ulcers, migraine headaches, low-back pain, psoriasis, and spastic colitis. It is a common belief among medical practitioners that at least 50 percent of all patients seen by physicians suffer from some underlying mental or emotional disorder. How much of this is due to toxic anger?

A few years ago my colleagues and I conducted a research project at Duke University Medical Center on the effects of personality patterns and life stress on ischemic cerebrovascular disease (stroke).[4] Among other questions, we asked both the patients hospitalized for stroke and our control patients, who were there for other medical reasons, about their emotional state at the time they became ill. They listed a range of emotions, including anger, sadness, shame, guilt, loneliness, and anxiety. However, the emotion most often experienced prior to the onset of illness was anger. Fifty-four percent of the stroke patients admitted to being angry immediately preceding the onset of symptoms.

The best evidence that toxic anger can shorten a person's life expectancy comes from studies of heart disease. Earlier I mentioned a study by Dr. Kawachi and his colleagues at the Harvard School of Public Health in which it was found that people in the highest category of anger were at a 60 percent greater risk for nonfatal heart attacks.[5] Even more important, Dr. Kawachi found that the likelihood of survival over an eight-

> As intense as my anger was every day for two years, it's amazing I didn't have a heart attack. I was saved from that fate, I guess, by the fact that I was under fifty years of age, I'm not overweight, I've never smoked, I have low cholesterol, and there's no family history of heart disease. What I had instead was an emotional heart attack.

year follow-up period depended on how angry these men were when they were first interviewed.

It is interesting that Dr. Kawachi's high-anger patients also tended to smoke more, weigh more, and consume more alcohol, suggesting that anger may also play an indirect role in causing heart attacks through substance abuse and overeating. As you recall, this is exactly what my coworkers and I found in our community survey (Chapter 2).

Other researchers have shown that toxic anger may eventually lead to coronary death in cases of *myocardial ischemia,* or reduced blood supply to the heart muscle.[6] High levels of anger have been shown to act as a "proximate trigger" of ischemia, with the same effect as strenuous physical activity or cigarette smoking. Ischemia was twice as likely to occur in heart patients with high self-ratings of anger as in those with low self-ratings. The heart rates associated with the onset of ischemia in "high-anger" patients were also higher than those of "low-anger" patients, suggesting a higher level of physiological demand on the heart. Anger-induced heart attacks tend to occur shortly after the person becomes angry, typically within two hours, and may explain many of the so-called sudden deaths. Whether toxic anger serves as a potential or actual trigger for life-threatening heart disease depends of course on the vulnerability of one's cardiovascular system.

Dr. Meyer Friedman, a cardiologist who has worked extensively on treating coronary risk associated with the Type A behavior pattern,

I'd be lying if I said I never seriously considered suicide when I got angry during my years of depression. It wasn't fear of dying or religious concerns that kept me from killing myself. I just didn't want to leave that legacy for my wife and children. When you turn that kind of rage on yourself, it can be scary.

warns of a potentially lethal process called *sludging*. This occurs when too much fat in the blood causes red blood cells to stick together and slows the flow of blood to the heart. "If you cannot keep from becoming irritated, aggravated, impatient, or angry," says Dr. Friedman, "at least have enough common sense to avoid food of any kind during or immediately after your emotional outburst."[7]

Many patients suffering from anger-induced ischemia also have smoked and abused caffeine and alcohol. In fact, additional studies suggest that many individuals may smoke in order to self-medicate anger. In one study of smoking cessation, all smokers who quit the program or ultimately relapsed were independently judged by a psychiatrist to be unusually angry people.[8] The smokers who completed the program and succeeded in remaining smoke-free were not. Intense anger is often cited as a major cause of smoker relapse.

Mental illness can also shorten one's life expectancy. A second way toxic anger affects longevity is through suicide. The "anger turned inward" that characterizes many depressed people is sometimes released in one extreme act of self-destructive behavior. Anger is no doubt the primary motivation for many adolescent suicides, but people of other age groups are just as vulnerable. For example, years ago I read a suicide note left by an elderly man who took his life by shooting himself in the head. The note, written to his wife of many years, said simply: "I hate you. Love, Harry."

In the case of extreme TAS, one's life can be cut short by the legal consequences of homicidal behavior. Professor Edwin Megargee, a psychologist at Florida State University, has devoted his career to studying the motives behind criminal violence. He has focused most of his attention on two distinct "types" of criminals: the undercontrolled and assaultive type and the chronically overcontrolled type. The first type is perhaps more familiar to us—the person who lashes out in anger frequently whenever he gets frustrated or mildly provoked. The second type is the "nice guy" who rarely gets angry for most of his life, then one day casually walks into a fast-food restaurant and guns down a dozen innocent people without warning. Both types end up on death row, and both are victims of toxic anger. The undercontrolled type experiences intense anger when provoked and feels few inhibitions, like anxiety or empathy, against acting out his anger through physical aggressiveness. Therefore, he acts violently. The overcontrolled type, on the other hand, experiences a buildup of unexpressed anger over time because of his strong inhibitions against aggressive behavior but eventually releases the anger in a single, often deadly, outrageous act. Many individuals on death row, according to Dr. Megargee, are there because of anger gone awry rather than motives such as greed or power, which he says are more typical of "professional 'hit men,' assassins, bank robbers, and arsonists."[9] Prison with the possibility of execution is a high price to pay for toxic anger!

◆ ◆ ◆

Dr. Glen Elder, a psychologist working at the University of North Carolina, has provided the best example of the impact of toxic anger on a person's educational, marital, parental, and occupational life. He and his colleagues conducted a longitudinal study of hundreds of ten-year-old middle-income children, some of whom were classified as *ill-tempered*.[10] The researchers followed and reevaluated these children throughout their adult years to age forty.

The children were classified as ill-tempered if they consistently engaged in angry temper tantrums involving both physical (biting, kicking, striking, and throwing things) and verbal (swearing, screaming, and shouting) explosions. Both the severity and the frequency of their tan-

My father was a smart man, but he never graduated from high school. They say he got into a fight with another student two days before graduation and ended up hitting the principal when he tried to intervene. The principal retaliated by not letting my father graduate with his class. He never went back to get his degree.

It would be easy to say that one incident changed my father's whole life, but it didn't. By all accounts, it was just one of many losses he experienced because of his bad temper. He lost jobs, a loving wife, friends, the respect of his children, and eventually his health. He lost everything because of anger.

trums were taken into account, the latter ranging from once a month to several times each day. Of the hundreds of children studied, 28 percent of the boys and 32 percent of the girls fit this pattern of ill-tempered behavior.

Elder and his colleagues believed that these ill-tempered children were "moving against the world," demonstrating an interactional style that had serious long-term social consequences. These youngsters had failed to master a fundamental social requirement when handling frustration or responding to adult authority: "the need to delay gratification, control impulses, and modulate emotional expression."

What were the long-term social consequences? The ill-tempered boys subsequently became ill-tempered men who often terminated their formal education early, found themselves in jobs of lower rank and status than those of their fathers (at the same age), and had difficulty maintaining stable employment compared to their even-tempered peers. These men, in effect, experienced what sociologists call downward social mobility at a time when most middle-income Americans were moving upward in the world. Not only were their work lives erratic but their marital lives were as well. Twice as many of these men were divorced by age forty compared to their even-tempered peers.

For the women, the long-term effects of being an ill-tempered child were primarily felt in their marriages and families. Elder observed that "ill-temperedness in childhood not only consigned these women to marriages 'below their station,' it also contributed to the deterioration of these relationships." As in the men's group, twice as many of the ill-tempered women had divorced by midlife compared to their even-tempered peers. In most instances of intact marriages, there was significantly more conflict between husbands and wives. Furthermore, the ill-tempered girls became ill-tempered mothers and were perceived by both their husbands and children as inadequate parents.

Not only are angry mothers more likely to behave abusively toward their children, but they are also less likely to allow their children the opportunity to freely exchange thoughts and feelings with them. In addition, these mothers are less likely to be effective problem-solvers for the family.

♦ ♦ ♦

Some years ago, I attended the inaugural meeting of a society of cardiovascular rehabilitation specialists, where I was rather stunned to hear the keynote speaker, a cardiologist of international acclaim, state unequivocally that "the greatest medical and social problem facing us in the decades ahead is loneliness." Like all the other medical professionals in attendance, I was expecting the usual speech about the well-documented advantages of proper diet, moderate exercise, and not smoking in relation to cardiovascular health and longevity. Instead, we were told of the health-enhancing effects of establishing and maintaining effective social relationships. We were told that a loss of intimacy with our fellow humans could, in fact, promote serious illness and shorten our lives.

The speaker's message proved prophetic. Dr. Redford Williams and his colleagues at Duke University Medical Center proved years later, in a study of 1,368 patients who had undergone coronary angiography, that being married or having a "confidant" was predictive of survival over a five-year follow-up period.[11] Patients were asked five simple questions:

Are you presently marrried?

Do you have as much social contact as you would like with friends and relatives?

Are your family relationships satisfying; that is, do you get along well with members of your family and do you find your interactions with them rewarding?

Do you have as much contact as you would like with someone you feel close to, someone you can trust and confide in?

Do you find yourself feeling lonely often?

Patients who answered "no" to these questions were more than three times more likely to die from heart disease within five years compared to those who answered "yes." This striking difference in survival rates was sustained even when the investigators took into account the severity of heart disease found in each patient.

One major reason that many coronary patients feel isolated and lonely is that they suffer from toxic anger. People are generally repelled by anger that occurs too often, is too intense, and lasts too long. I've described David's daughter, who quickly ran to her room whenever her father got angry; Carl, the twenty-eight-year-old man whose wife took the kids to her parents' home when he lost his temper; and John, who felt like an outsider even around those he loved most. As he said, "You lose a lot of friends when you're that angry. You don't make friends as easy."

Toxic anger often causes the angry person to terminate relationships with the people who anger him. Remember Joe? He ended his friendship with his coworker Stephen because he was angry that Stephen received the promotion that Joe believed was rightfully his.

Toxic anger stifles social exchange. It causes the angry person and everyone around him or her to retreat into a protective, defensive silence that fosters estrangement among all parties.

I can't tell you how many friendships I've walked away from because of anger. George was a close friend of many years who said no when I asked if my family and I could spend the night at his home on our way out of Texas. Richard was a colleague with whom I had worked closely for years who wrote me a letter that upset me when I was at the peak of my depression. And Daryl, one of the most interesting and compassionate people I've ever known, scolded my secretary and made her cry. One moment of intense anger in each case, and I lost three of the best friends I've ever had. That's all it took.

The man joined his relatives in the restaurant and, with an angry tone, immediately asked to see the manager. He was clearly upset. "I called here twenty minutes ago and asked your employee Eddie to check and see if there were people named Greene seated in the smoking section," he loudly explained. "He said there weren't. And now I find out they've been here for quite a while waiting on me. That makes me really mad!"

"I can understand that, sir," the manager replied, "but you see, Eddie works the other location, which you must have called by mistake." The man looked away in silence, while the manager excused himself. One of the women at the table giggled, and the man barked at her, "Don't laugh. It isn't funny!" After that, they all sat in stony silence, while the angry man stared out the window waiting for his breakfast.

Toxic anger can be expensive. The most obvious and immediate costs relate to property damage.

A man becomes angry because his wife asks him to stop at the drugstore on their way out of town for vacation. He's in a hurry and wants to get on the road. As he leaves the drugstore, he backs into another car. He damages his brand-new car and has to pay the $100 deductible.

A college student gets angry at his girlfriend and smashes his fist through the wall of his apartment. His hand is fine, but the landlord charges $200 to have the wall repaired.

A teenage girl, angry at her parents, kicks a hole in her bedroom door. Her father makes her buy a new door that costs $93.

There are also medical and legal costs associated with destructive anger. Consider the thousand dollars Jeffrey and his parents spent to repair his broken hand. Peter incurred huge legal costs after he brutally abused his fourteen-month-old daughter. Also take into account the cost of cigarettes and alcohol used to self-medicate high levels of anger. Or the cost of a heart attack, hiatal hernia, or high blood pressure caused by toxic anger.

Finally, there is the cost of lost time from work resulting from TAS. In a recent study of more than eighty employees at a correctional facility, my colleagues and I found that employees who scored high on TA were three times more likely to have missed time from work because of illness in the past three months than were those who reported nontoxic levels of anger.

♦ ♦ ♦

After you have identified the personal costs associated with toxic anger, your attitude about changing this aspect of your emotional life should be more intentional. You should now be ready to begin a self-help program aimed at *detoxifying* your anger. All you need now is a little support.

EXERCISE

WHAT IS ANGER COSTING YOU?

Using the example in Figure 6-1, construct a pie chart of the costs associated with your toxic anger. Include all categories that you think are relevant: health/medical, occupational, educational, social/interpersonal, legal, and financial. The larger the piece, the more significant the cost of anger in that area.

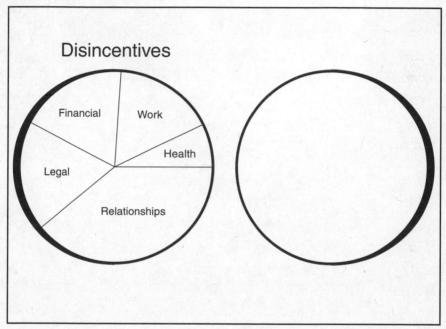

Can you think of other costs that I have not discussed? If so, what are they?

_____

_____

_____

_____

CHAPTER 7

TEAM BUILDING

The loneliness of man is the loneliness of the animal.
We must have each other. . . .
The animal cannot stand alone.
—Robert Ardrey, *The Social Contract*

Behavioral change is difficult, but without support from others it may be altogether impossible. The question should not be "Do I need support in order to free myself from toxic anger?" but, rather, "How much support do I need and where can I get it?" This chapter is intended to help you identify a support team—what I like to refer to as your *anger allies*—to assist you in detoxifying your anger.

♦ ♦ ♦

Some years ago, I was asked to speak at a meeting of a support group for persons afflicted with multiple sclerosis (MS) and their families. Like toxic anger, MS is a complex health problem that must be treated both biologically and psychologically. If MS sufferers are to have any chance of coping with the rigors of the disease and maintaining a meaningful and productive life, they must have the help of others.

I began my remarks by asking for a show of hands from those people at the meeting who had MS. All the MS patients responded, along with a few family members. I pointed to one young man who had not raised his hand and asked, "Sir, do you have MS?" His face quickly reddened as he answered defensively, "No! My wife is the one with MS." As fate would have it, his wife was the person who had invited me to speak and was now standing by my side.

"Oh, so your wife has the disease," I continued. "Yes," he replied. "But you have your wife, right?" I said. "Well, yes," he answered hesitantly. "Well, then, if your wife has MS and you have your wife, it seems to me that you too have MS. Am I right?" I countered. The man fell silent and turned his head away.

In that moment, I could sense the lonely struggle this poor woman was facing with her illness. I could sense the immense isolation she felt standing there in a room full of people. I could see the painful lack of support in her tearful expression. And I could feel her husband's anger all the way across the room.

SUPPORT IS MANY THINGS

There is a tendency to think of support primarily in emotional terms, as an expression of compassion or "reaching out" by some caring individual. However, Dr. James House of the University of Michigan offers a more comprehensive definition. Support is "a flow of one or more of four things between people: (a) emotional concern, (b) instrumental aid, (c) information, and/or (d) appraisal."[1]

There is no question that *emotional concern* is the most important type of support a person needs to change maladaptive behavior effectively. But there is also no question that this may be the most difficult type of support for the person with toxic anger to receive. As you might imagine, it is hard for most people to love, care for, and reach out to the person suffering from toxic anger when they have repeatedly been on the receiving end of that person's wrath. In the last chapter, I discussed how toxic anger stifles social exchange and ends relationships. However, anger not only shrinks the size of the person's social network, but also interrupts the two-way "flow" between people through which human beings give and receive support. David, the fifty-five-year-old angry man with chronic back pain, is a prime example. Over the years, his family learned to avoid his anger by literally avoiding him much of the time. "I can tell when he's angry," his daughter said, "and I just go to my room." This young woman clearly loved her father, but she was unable to express this love because she was afraid that his anger might erupt at any moment.

The other three types of support—instrumental aid, information, and appraisal—are equally as important. *Instrumental aid* entails doing something tangible for the angry person. A young college student who came for treatment of toxic anger, for example, did not have a way to get to my office. He did not have a car, and my office was not reachable by public transportation. At first he considered holding off treatment, but finally he asked a friend to bring him for his weekly sessions. To his surprise, his friend was more than glad to help. If someone buys you a book on anger management or pays for you to receive professional treatment, that is an example of instrumental or tangible support.

Some years ago a man brought his sixteen-year-old son to see me for problems with intense anger that had resulted in a growing pattern of delinquent behaviors—truancy, drug use, and fighting at school—as well as increasing family tension. The boy's problems had begun after his parents' divorce several years earlier and seemed more pronounced now that he was a teenager. The father loved his son but was not terribly expressive emotionally. However, he was willing to take time from work to bring his son to therapy, pay for treatment, and also pay for him to enroll in both martial arts and theater classes, which I had suggested as outlets for his pent-up anger. The tangible support his father provided was vital to the success we achieved in turning this boy's emotional life around.

Informational support involves advice or guidance about what one can do to recognize and treat maladaptive anger. The anger screening that my wife and I conducted at our local health and safety fair is an example. Self-help books, pamphlets, and audio- and videotapes on the topic of anger all provide informational support. They let you know that help is available, and they offer a "game plan" for detoxifying your anger.

> Tom listened to my anger sometimes for hours. He didn't encourage it, nor did he condemn it. He just listened. He didn't try to be my therapist. He didn't pretend to have all the answers to my problems. He was just a good friend, which is what I needed most.

This type of support can also be provided by legal and medical professionals, who typically become aware of the costs and consequences of toxic anger long before the problem finds its way into the hands of a trained mental health professional.

The last type of support, *appraisal*, involves giving people with toxic anger feedback both about the inappropriateness of their anger and about any improvement—no matter how small—one might observe as a result of their efforts to diminish their anger. Getting honest, constructive feedback about your anger either before or after you embark on a program of change may be difficult, however. Those closest to you, who are in the best position to evaluate your behavior critically, may be the least likely to offer feedback. They may be afraid of making you madder than you already are or they may feel resentment toward you for making their lives hell, which makes it difficult for them to see positive change when it does occur.

◆ ◆ ◆

List some people you think will support you in your efforts to detoxify your anger. Beside each name, list the type of support you have received or are likely to receive from that person (emotional, tangible, informational, feedback), and give an example of how that type of support has been or might be expressed by that individual.

SOCIAL SUPPORT

Source	Type	Method of Expression
Nancy	E	Lets me ventilate.
My mother	T	Will keep kids when I'm too stressed.
Jason	I	Gave me a magazine article on anger.

ANGER SUPPORT GROUPS

Support groups are immensely helpful for people seeking to change some aspect of their behavior. For one thing, support groups promote a feeling of *universality:* People suffering from toxic anger are for the first time exposed to "kindred souls" struggling more or less successfully with the same problem. Support groups also provide angry people with a type of *credible feedback* from others who share their problem. Group members feel less defensive and can share more openly among their angry peers.

Unfortunately, there may not be any anger support groups currently available in your community, again owing to the fact that toxic anger has yet to be identified as a problem in its own right. However, you can start one yourself. Remember that support groups differ from therapy groups primarily in that the latter must be led by a trained professional. Support groups, on the other hand, simply involve two or more untrained people who share a common problem and who are willing to meet regularly for the purpose of supporting each other in one or more of the four ways previously suggested.

◆ ◆ ◆

See if your community offers anger support groups by

1. Checking the listing of community support groups in your local newspaper

2. Calling your local mental health clinic or health department to inquire about such groups
3. Checking with any local mental health practitioners (clinical psychologists, psychiatrists, social workers) to see if they know about such groups

SPONSORSHIP

Another way to obtain support for the changes you are trying to make in anger is through a process referred to in Alcoholics Anonymous as *sponsorship*.[2] Sponsorship involves a one-to-one relationship between you and some other person who has already been successful in eliminating toxic anger from his or her life. Sponsorship is about mutual and confidential sharing between two people centered around a common problem. The qualities and behaviors that make someone a good sponsor include the following:

♦ They show by personal example how to live a life free of toxic anger.
♦ They actively listen and encourage you in all your efforts to bring anger under control.
♦ They are nonjudgmental and accept you as you are.
♦ They do not pretend to have all the answers, realizing that toxic anger is a complex problem that differs greatly from one person to another.
♦ They keep in regular contact, by phone or in person, and whenever possible are available when you are in an emotional crisis.
♦ They do not impose their personal views, understanding that what worked for them may not necessarily work for you.
♦ They do not try to be responsible for your toxic anger, leaving that responsibility instead where it rightfully belongs—in your hands.

+ They are patient, flexible, and honest in their efforts to help you.
+ They are compassionate but do not pity you.
+ They do not hesitate to encourage you to get professional help if needed.

People who have difficulty trusting other people or who are not comfortable disclosing personal information in a group setting may find sponsorship a much more attractive option in terms of support.

In Chapter 2, I related the story of a young man, Peter, who broke his fourteen-month-old daughter's arms in a moment of extreme anger. One wonders if that tragic incident could have been prevented if Peter had a sponsor he could have called when he first began to lose control of his temper. Someone may have been able to give him advice at that "critical moment" about how to stop the child from crying in a safe and effective way without the use of physical violence. With that type of support, he might not have lost custody of his daughter and forever been labeled a child abuser.

◆ ◆ ◆

Write down the names of three people you think qualify as anger sponsors:

_____

_____

_____

TWO FINAL THOUGHTS

On a final note, I caution you in two respects: First, *do not try to get all your support needs met by one person.* No single individual, even under the best of circumstances, can meet all our support needs all the time. If someone tries to do this, he or she is likely to get burned out from overuse. Diversify—the more anger allies the better! Second, *remember that social support needs to be reciprocal.* As the saying goes, "what goes around comes around." You need to acknowledge and reinforce those who are on your team. You need to let them know that the changes you are trying to make would not be possible without their help. Don't underestimate the power of a simple "thank you"!

♦ ♦ ♦

Now that you have identified toxic anger as a problem, are sufficiently motivated, and have constructed a support team, you are finally ready to embark on a program of change. The next ten chapters outline a series of steps you can take to become effective at detoxifying your anger. It is important to keep in mind that no one step by itself will solve your anger problem. The ultimate solution to your toxic anger problem lies in the combination of these ten strategies that best fits your particular situation. I suggest you read all ten chapters and then decide on a game plan. Good luck!

CHAPTER 8

MIRROR, MIRROR ON THE WALL

"Queen, you are full fair,'tis true,
But Snow-White is fairer than you." . . .
and from that hour her heart turned
against Snow-White and she hated her.
—Brothers Grimm

Toxic anger all too often mirrors certain fundamental, albeit faulty, presumptions about life that define an individual's basic personality. *Presumptions* are the beliefs, values, and expectations that we take for granted and, in effect, bring to everyday life situations. *Personality*, as I use the term here, refers to how people generally see themselves in relation to others. It is this particular set of presumptions about "self versus other" that makes each person unique. Toxic anger as reflected in the self is an expression of one or more distorted, irrational "self-versus-other" concepts. In the following four sections, I describe the personality types that are most likely to experience toxic anger.

NARCISSISTIC PERSONALITY

Like the evil queen in the fable *Snow White*, many people view themselves not just as "full fair" but as the "fairest of them all." They have an exalted sense of self that includes elements of both *grandiosity* ("I can be or do anything I want!") and *perfectionism* ("I must do no wrong!"). More important, they presume that everyone else shares their "special" view of themself and will, therefore, grant them license to behave as they please because of these qualities. In psychiatry, we call such individuals *narcissists* after the mythological Greek figure Narcissus, who fell in love with his own image while gazing into a fountain.

Narcissists value their own needs above those of all other people. As noted psychoanalyst Dr. Theodore Rubin put it, "the narcissist becomes his own world and believes the whole world is him."[1] They believe "ordinary" people in the world are there simply to affirm and satisfy their special needs, whether emotional, financial, or relational. Other people are allowed to have and satisfy needs only in so far as their needs do not conflict with or take away from those of the narcissist. As long as the narcissist is satisfied, there is no problem.

What happens when others do not live up to narcissists' unrealistic expectations or when some change in life circumstances (accident, disease, death, being fired, divorce) interferes with narcissists' efforts to maintain their special status? They become angry—extremely angry—often to the point of uncontrollable rage. Sometimes this rage is directed outward. A beauty pageant queen, for example, angrily assaults her ex-boyfriend's father after she is rejected. The leader of a juvenile gang critically wounds a college student in a drive-by shooting after being turned away from a party. A teenage girl kicks in her bedroom door when her parents tell her she cannot go on "beach week" with her friends.

Other times, the anger is directed inward. Barbara was sixty-seven years old when I first met her. She had been a feisty, energetic woman who worked on an assembly line in a local factory by choice rather than economic necessity. She had prided herself in being the most productive employee on the line and enjoyed the special recognition this afforded her. However, because of a work injury, she was no longer employed. Instead, she spent her days at home alone, complaining of pain, severely depressed, and threatening suicide. She was such a nice "little old lady"; who would have believed that underneath all that depression and disability was a cauldron of rage? "That's not me!" she would angrily protest, mourning the loss of her former self. Barabara no longer saw herself as "special."

Not only is there an overemphasis on the self with narcissism, but there is also an exaggerated sense of *entitlement*. Narcissists do not simply prefer to have their way in life; they literally demand it. It is not enough to compete in an effort to win; the narcissist *must* be the winner. The narcissist must be adored by all, must be perfect in everything that she does, and must always be right or she will become consumed by anger.

Narcissistic anger is typically vengeful and designed to hurt the offending party. The wicked queen in Snow White demanded no less from the huntsman: "Take the child out into the woods, so that I may set eyes on her no more. You must put her to death, and bring me her heart for a token."

♦ ♦ ♦

Do the following self-statements sound all too familiar?

"They can't do that to *ME*!"

"*I* know what *I'm* doing. *I* don't need anyone criticizing *ME*!"

"*I* did a damned good job. He owes *ME* that raise!"

"It's not fair. *I* deserved to win!"

"They didn't give *ME* a chance!"

"Do you know how much you've hurt *ME*!"

"How dare you treat *ME* that way!"

"Hurry up, people. You're making *ME* late!"

"Get out of *MY* way, buddy!"

"Do you know how long *I've* been sitting here!"

Recall the customer in the restaurant who repeatedly yelled at the busy waitress, "*My* coffee's cold! *I* want some hot coffee!," or the wealthy executive who assaulted his wife when she "let the kids drink all the orange juice, leaving none for *my* breakfast." Now do you understand why these men were so angry?

CYNICAL PERSONALITY

Cynicism reflects a pervasive attitude of mistrust regarding the motives of others. Cynics presume they will be treated unfairly and unjustly in most instances and have little faith in the inherent goodness of other people. Rather, they view the world as a dangerous place full of traps and pitfalls where one must constantly be on guard if one is to survive. Because they anticipate being victimized, cynics are always ready to respond in an angry, defensive manner.

Renting a truck to help your daughter move sounds like a simple task. Not so for Anthony. From the time he left the rental agency, he worried *they* would unfairly charge him for damage done to the truck by previous renters. After all, *they* had his credit card information and it would be *their* word against his. Throughout the day, when he wasn't loading or unloading furniture, he inspected the truck, looking for evidence of damage *they* could wrongly attribute to him. He found himself getting increasingly irritated as he thought about being unjustly charged for something he had not done. "If *they* give me any trouble," he finally decided, "I'll stop payment on the charge card and then call my lawyer. *They*'re not going to get over on me!" In the end, the people at the rental agency were very nice, and Anthony was left "stewing in his own juices."

> The longer we wait for our food in a restaurant, the more I find myself wondering if the people who came in after us are getting their food first. The longer we wait in line for a show, the more I think "maybe we won't get a seat or it'll be sold out." Once I start thinking that way, I can feel myself getting upset, tense, and angry. It takes all the fun out of everything.

There is a moral or righteous justification to cynical anger. Cynics believe people clearly deserve what they get! The cynic, after all, is the "good guy" who is simply trying to survive in a world of "bad guys."

♦ ♦ ♦

A prime example of how a cynical attitude can lead to toxic anger and consequently poor health is found in the Type A personality. Cardiologists Meyer Friedman and Ray Rosenman first coined the term *Type A* in the late 1950s to describe a pattern of pathological behavior that greatly increased the risk of heart disease.[2] Their initial efforts were focused on the more obvious, observable characteristics of Type A behavior: time urgency, a slavish devotion to work, and a hard-driving orientation to life. However, Dr. Virginia Price, one of their colleagues at the Harold Brunn Institute in San Francisco, subsequently pointed out that cynicism characterized the core beliefs underlying Type A behavior. According to Dr. Price, Type A's are motivated by fears that "good may not prevail" and "justice may not triumph," as well as the presumption that their "well-being is always in jeopardy."[3] What others see as hostile, hard-driving, and achievement-striving behavior is, in effect, the Type A individual's way of coping with cynicism. The anger seen in Type A people is typically vengeful. Type A's are not just letting off steam or trying to exert authority or independence with their anger; they are attempting to ensure that justice will prevail. Once justice has been restored, they can relax, but only until the next injustice occurs!

CATASTROPHIC PERSONALITY

I use the term *catastrophic* to refer to *a great or sudden disaster; a complete misfortune or ruin*. The person afflicted with a catastrophic mind-set falsely presumes that all problems in life, all inconveniences, all unforeseen stresses, regardless of magnitude, are cause for great and grave concern. The alarm sounds, there is a surge of adrenaline, and the "catastrophic self" is flooded with emotion, in this case toxic anger. In his book *Anger: How to Live With and Without It,* psychologist Albert Ellis explains how people's tendency to "awfulize" the everyday circumstances of their lives can lead to irrational and excessive anger.[4] Many people, according to Dr. Ellis, "seem to have a tendency to equate unfair, inconvenient, or disadvantageous with awful." Clearly, it is fair to feel inconvenienced when the person in line ahead of you takes longer than you think is necessary to complete his purchase; however, to perceive this delay to be an "awful waste of my time" demonstrates the catastrophic mind-set. Whereas the former might lead to a feeling of annoyance, the latter will almost assuredly provoke full-fledged anger.

This tendency to catastrophize—embellish, magnify, or exaggerate the importance of a minor provocation—coupled with the tendency to "respond in kind" more than anything else determines the intensity with which anger is experienced. If the perception of harm is exaggerated, so too is the angry response.

How often do you find yourself thinking or saying out loud words like:

"She treated me just *awful!*"

"That was a *terrible* thing to do!"

"I can't believe he would say such *horrible* things!"

"This is *awful*! Now, I'm going to be late."

"He made me feel *horrible*. I just hate him!"

Too often?

COMPULSIVE PERSONALITY

John, the ex-Marine discussed previously, is a man of strong moral and ethical principles. He believes in God, the sanctity of marriage, the American way of life, and the value of hard work. He believes there is a right and a wrong way to do everything: cut wood, mow grass, fix a car. In his world, people are either good or bad. They are good if they see things his way, bad if they don't. There is no middle ground!

John likes order in his life. He lives by strict rules, and he has little tolerance for people who do not see things his way. Those who know him best see him as stubborn and persistent. "He always has to be right, and, believe me, his word is final!" his wife said.

John hates change. He is always punctual. He is "tight" with his money. He knows how to work hard, but he has little experience just having fun. He likes cutting wood and doing "mechanical" things.

John is an example of a compulsive personality. By compulsive, I do not mean being busy all the time or always engaged in getting things done. In a psychiatric sense, *compulsive* refers to a rigid, narrow-minded way of thinking about and dealing with the world. Everything is either black or white; there are no gray areas. Although they are not cynical about life, compulsive people are far too serious for their own good. Work is essential; play is optional. Compulsive people lack spontaneity. Everything must be organized, planned, and on schedule. Any deviation from the plan, any interruption in the schedule, leads to frustration and anger. They are masters of detail, but they often fail to grasp the "big picture" of what is going on in their lives. A compulsive parent, for example, may become upset when his teenage child expresses views different from his own rather than seeing this as a logical first step toward independence and eventual adulthood. A compulsive employer may become upset if employees show initiative or creativity, insisting instead that they "just do as they are told." Compulsive individuals keep a tight rein not only on their finances but on their emotions as well. And when they do lose emotional control, it is typically expressed as irritation.

John, of course, is by no means unique. Dennis, the depressed middle-aged executive who worked his way up from the rank of accountant to president, also had a compulsive personality. Peter, the young man who physically abused his infant daughter because she would not stop crying, was compulsive as well. The man in the restaurant who chided his companions for laughing at his mistake also fit this personality type.

> I was getting more and more angry. Here I was on Saturday morning stacking a dump truck load of wood, and there was my teenaged son twenty feet away from me playing basketball. "He should be helping me with all this work that needs to be done around here," I told myself, "not spending his time playing. Can't he see that!"
>
> Then, all of a sudden, it hit me. There's something wrong with this picture. I'm doing all the work, and he's having all the fun. Something needs to change.
>
> So I said to my son, "Give me a hand with this wood, and I'll play some ball with you, okay?" He agreed, and we spent the rest of the morning working and playing together.
>
> And my anger? It all went away. . . .

SELF-ASSESSMENT (IF THE SHOE FITS . . .)

Now that you have a clearer understanding of the personality traits that underlie toxic anger, you are ready for self-assessment. Think about what you have just read and the examples I have provided, which illustrate each of these personality types, and then rate yourself on the following scales. If a particular label seems to fit you "moderately" or "extremely" well, write down a few examples demonstrating why you think this is true. Remember to be honest with yourself; otherwise the exercise will be meaningless. After you have rated yourself, have one or more members of your support team (anger allies) rate you as well. It is always helpful to have an outside objective opinion.

NARCISSISTIC

1	2	3	4
Not at all	Somewhat	Moderately	Extremely

Examples:

_____

_____

_____

_____

CYNICAL

1	2	3	4
Not at all	Somewhat	Moderately	Extremely

Examples:

_____

_____

_____

_____

CATASTROPHIC

1	2	3	4
Not at all	Somewhat	Moderately	Extremely

Examples:

_____

_____

_____

_____

COMPULSIVE

1	2	3	4
Not at all	Somewhat	Moderately	Extremely

Examples:

_____

_____

_____

You need to be concerned only with the scales on which you rated yourself, or were rated by others, as either a 3 or a 4. It is these areas in which you are most vulnerable to excessive anger. Were you high on more than one scale? Was your total score (of the four scales combined) higher than 8? If so, the solutions that follow will prove especially helpful. Your scores here will assist in choosing the solutions that best fit your anger problem.

If you did not score high on any of the four toxic personality scales— *good for you!* The reasons for your TAS will be found in later chapters.

THE THREE R'S

1. *Reject* the notion that one point of view—one way of perceiving, judging, and reacting to the world around you—fits all life situations. Without a doubt, the major "flaw" in the day-to-day think-

ing of anger-prone personalities is the distorted belief that *everyone* must see them as special, that *everyone* is tricky and deceitful, that *every* problem is a crisis, or that *everyone* should be as serious about life as they are. Life is more complex than that!

2. *Recognize* the fact that other people you know and with whom you interact daily do not suffer from toxic anger because they do not see the world as you do. They have a much more balanced perspective on life; things are black *and* white and sometimes gray!

3. *Realize* that it is never too late to change your mind. You can begin choosing alternative, nontoxic ways of viewing the world at any point in your life. The adage "you can't teach an old dog new tricks" is simply untrue!

EXERCISES

The letter codes (*N* = narcissistic, *Cy* = cynical, *Ca* = catastrophic, *Co* = compulsive) preceding each exercise indicate which personality type will be helped by that specific exercise.

N. Tape-record a conversation between you and someone you know who is not burdened with toxic anger. Play it back and count how many self-reference (I, me, mine) statements you made throughout. Then count the number of self-reference statements made by the other person. If you had a significantly higher count, try cutting back on your use of such statements. Try alternating self-reference statements ("I think . . .") with other-reference statements ("My wife thinks . . .") for a change.

Co. Once a month, plan a weekend of *non*accomplishment. Make a detailed list of all the things you and your family "should" do that weekend and then burn the list in ceremonial fashion. Use the time instead to get to know one another and play together. Try having a forty-eight-hour

> If I had taken this test five years ago, I would have been a 15. No wonder I was so angry all the time! Today, I'm an 8.
>
> I'm not the same person I was for the past twenty years. Catherine and the kids can see I've changed, but I know they still expect "my old angry self" to return whenever there's a family crisis of some kind. I don't blame them for not completely trusting this change in my personality; twenty years is a long time.

movie marathon: no interruptions, no chores, just movies day and night. Or start out on Saturday morning on a two-day trip with no particular destination. See where the road takes you, and stop and explore everything that looks the least bit interesting.

Cy. Start a scrapbook of clippings from newspapers and household magazines about good and faith-affirming events: A man returns a wallet full of money to its rightful owner. Motorists on a busy freeway stop to aid an injured dog. A woman of modest means establishes a scholarship fund at a major university for underprivileged students. Add to your scrapbook several times a week.

Cy. Don't overexpose yourself to television news shows that focus on the negative, unjust side of life. This only reinforces a cynical outlook.

N. Make a point of periodically engaging in activities in which you are not the center of attention. For example, work backstage on a local theater production or volunteer in an important but menial capacity (park cars, collect trash, sell popcorn) at a community-sponsored event.

Co. Practice not having the last word in an argument. Let the other person have the final word, but you decide when that is. You may find you have more control this way. When should you let the other person have the last word? Just as soon as you begin to feel yourself getting irritated or aroused!

Ca. Develop a 10-point classification system similar to the Richter scale to measure stressful life events:

Less than 3.5 = Not felt but recorded
3.5–5.4   = Often felt, minor damage
5.5–6.0   = Slight damage
6.1–6.9   = Can be moderately destructive
7.0–7.9   = Serious damage
8.0 and above = Total destruction

A 1.0 earthquake (minor) has the energy equivalent of six ounces of TNT; a 5.0 earthquake (moderate), 200 tons of TNT; and an 8.0 quake (major), approximately 6.3 million tons of TNT. The same variation in magnitude holds true for the stressors of everyday life. Many are barely felt, whereas others are indeed earth-shaking!

N, Cy, Ca, Co. Challenge your anger-provoking thoughts, beliefs, and expectations. Try to find alternative (less self-centered, less mistrusting, less catastrophic, less rigid) ways of interpreting events that tend to upset you regularly:

Narcissistic thought: "Why are all these people in *my* way?"

Nonnarcissistic alternative: "I'm sure these folks probably have important things to do today just like I do. Unfortunately, we're all trying to do them at the same time."

Cynical thought: "That idiot pulled out in front of me *on purpose!*"

Noncynical alternative: "That guy didn't pull out in front of me on purpose; he just doesn't know how to drive very well."

Catastrophic thought: "I got a *terrible* grade on my term paper."

Noncatastrophic alternative: "I didn't get the grade I wanted on my paper. I'll have to talk to the professor and see what I can do to improve it."

Compulsive thought: "You're mowing the grass *all wrong!*"

Noncompulsive alternative: "You certainly aren't mowing the grass the way I do; but hey, you're mowing it."

N, Cy, Co. Try to stop thinking about the world in pluralistic (they, people, everything) terms. You are less likely to feel outnumbered and overwhelmed if you stick to he, she, and it. You will have less reason to be on the defensive.

N, Cy, Co. Eliminate inflammatory language from your vocabulary. This includes both overly demanding (should, ought to, have to, must) and critical (idiot, stupid, jerk, fool) words and phrases.

◆ ◆ ◆

Does your personality play a significant role in your toxic anger? If so, indicate it on the Toxic Anger Checklist on page 50.

CHAPTER 9

GIVE IT A REST

The only way to keep your health is to . . .
do what you'd rather not.
—Mark Twain

Stress and anger go hand and hand.

Alice was afraid she was turning out just like her mother. "She is such an angry woman!" she said. Alice was thirty-eight and a single parent to two young boys. She was divorced from her alcoholic husband, who had abandoned her four years earlier. She liked her job at the advertising agency where she worked, but she was exhausted every day. She admitted that working long hours helped keep her mind off all her problems. In addition, she felt guilty if she wasn't constantly doing something!

Alice had trouble getting to sleep most nights because she couldn't relax, and her sleep was frequently disturbed by angry thoughts from her past. She complained of tension headaches, and she felt restless and keyed up much of the time. She was unhappy and lonely.

Alice experienced anger almost every day. Little things would set her off. Her anger was so intense at times that she found herself "ranting and raving, screaming, throwing things, totally losing control." Sometimes it took days for her anger to subside.

Most of her anger was directed at her children. "I try and keep my cool at work," she said, "but even that is getting hard to do lately."

◆ ◆ ◆

Alice was an overstressed woman. She had too much responsibility on her shoulders, too much unresolved pain and anger from her past, too many recent changes in her life, too few friends who cared about her, and too little time for herself. Her mind and body were literally crying out for her to stop, slow down, catch her breath, take stock of her life, feel pain, admit she needed help, and cope with her problems instead of always running away from them.

Alice was suffering from stress overload ("toxic" stress), and she was showing signs of physical and emotional strain. Because her nervous system was too excited, she had trouble sleeping; she felt both keyed up and exhausted at the same time. These stressors explain why her anger was so out of control.

EMOTIONAL STRAIN

Dr. Walter B. Cannon, the noted Harvard researcher mentioned in Chapter 4, first applied the engineering principles of "stress and strain" to human physiology in 1935.[1] In his classic paper entitled "Stresses and Strains of Homeostasis," Cannon described how the nervous system functions to preserve a stable internal environment, which he called *homeostasis*. In essence, homeostasis represents the nervous system at rest. Stress, according to Cannon, was any departure from homeostasis, any state of excitation, or in effect the nervous system at work. Stress affected health by disturbing normal blood flow and interrupting adequate oxygen supply to the tissues, both of which contributed to disease and eventual death. Cannon noted that the nervous system was able to correct itself and return to homeostasis under conditions of normal or "standard" stress. But prolonged or severe stress led to a "breaking strain in the homeostatic mechanism."

Although Cannon was primarily concerned with physical strain— tense muscles, elevated blood pressure, increased heart rate—it is clear that stress can lead to emotional strain as well. Strain, in this sense, represents a distortion of the normal emotional responsiveness of an

> My new car only had three hundred miles on it when we drove up to a nearby city to see my alma mater play basketball. I was in an exceptionally good mood for a change, not my usual angry, depressed self. All that changed, however, when I returned from the game to find my car wrecked by a drunken college student. The actual damage wasn't bad, but I was emotionally devastated. I just stood there looking at the car, unable to respond. Our friends could see that something was wrong with me, so they took the kids home with them. Catherine tried to comfort me, but I just withdrew further and further into angry silence. I didn't say a single word to her all the way home—ninety miles. And then I immediately went to the office, where I stayed well into the night.

individual. When "normal" emotional experiences are exaggerated in frequency, intensity, and duration, the individual's response too is more extreme. Normal anxiety turns into panic. Sadness becomes depression. Annoyance and mild irritation escalate into toxic anger.

As discussed in Chapter 6, emotional strain experienced as intense anger appears to be one of the triggering mechanisms that leads to heart attacks and strokes.

MAJOR STRESS

Medical research on stress over the past half century has primarily focused on human reaction to major life events such as divorce, death, or serious illness, which always reflect a change in life circumstances and require a significant amount of emotional and behavioral adjustment. Although such events are typically not experienced on a daily basis, they tend to cluster or build up over time. Cannon, for example, talked about "developmental epochs," or stages of life, such as adolescence and old age, which he saw as potentially more stressful than others.

Psychiatrists Thomas H. Holmes and Richard H. Rahe developed a scale to measure people's stress level at any point in time by determining how many major life events they have been exposed to within the past twelve months.[2] The forty-three stress events on the scale are each assigned numerical ratings that measure their relative impact on homeostatic balance.

Write down the "impact value" assigned to each event you have experienced in the past year. If you have experienced a particular event more than once (e.g., two family members died, you lost your job more than once, you had twins, or you changed jobs four times), multiply the value of that event by the number of times you experienced it. Add up all the values to obtain your Total Major Events score:

Stress Events	Impact Score	Your Score
Death of spouse	100	_____
Divorce	73	_____
Marital separation	65	_____
Jail term	63	_____
Death of close family member	63	_____
Personal injury or illness	53	_____
Marriage	50	_____
Fired at work	47	_____
Marital reconciliation	45	_____
Retirement	45	_____
Change in health of family member	44	_____
Pregnancy	40	_____
Sex difficulties	39	_____
Gain of new family member	39	_____
Business readjustment	39	_____
Change in financial state	38	_____
Death of close friend	37	_____
Change in number of arguments with spouse	35	_____
Mortgage over $10,000	31	_____

Stress Events	Impact Score	Your Score
Foreclosure on mortgage or loan	30	_____
Change in responsibilities at work	29	_____
Son or daughter leaving home	29	_____
Trouble with in-laws	29	_____
Outstanding personal achievement	28	_____
Spouse begins or stops work	26	_____
Begin or end school	26	_____
Change in living conditions	25	_____
Revision of personal habits	24	_____
Trouble with boss	23	_____
Change in work hours or conditions	20	_____
Change in residence	20	_____
Change in schools	20	_____
Change in recreation	20	_____
Change in church activities	19	_____
Change in social activities	18	_____
Mortgage or loan less than $10,000	17	_____
Change in sleeping habits	16	_____
Change in number of family get-togethers	15	_____
Change in eating habits	15	_____
Vacation	13	_____
Christmas	12	_____
Minor violations of the law	11	_____
Total Major Events Stress Score =		_____

If your Total Stress score is below 150, the stress resulting from major life events is unlikely to play a significant role in your anger experience. If your score is between 150 and 299, you are experiencing above-average stress, which may spill over into toxic anger. If your score is 300 or above, your stress levels are above average and you are definitely a candidate for toxic anger.

> For ten years, before I had my nervous breakdown in 1988, I lived under unbelievable stress every day of my life. Two major career changes, two geographical moves, the death of both of my in-laws in less than two years, the agonizing death of my sister at age forty-two, the death of my dog, loss of my best friend, major debt for the first time in my life . . . and that's just the short list!
>
> The crazy part was that all that time I thought I was on top of things, that I was in control, that I was "okay." Boy, was I mistaken!

Alice was right when she said, "This has been the worst, most stressful year of my life." Her score was 2,292! She had been in and out of several significant relationships, had changed residence three times, had trouble with her boss on fifteen different occasions, had twice borrowed large sums of money that she had trouble paying back, and so on.

MINOR STRESS

Recent research has shown that it is often the minor day-to-day irritants of life, or hassles, that cause people to feel the most stressed. For one thing, minor stresses occur much more frequently than major ones. We do not, after all, get divorced every day, but we have to wait in line, fight with traffic, and deal with troublesome neighbors day in and day out. Second, because the minor events tend to have less immediate impact on us, we pay less attention to them. We "absorb" this type of stress more readily and do less to cope with it actively. Third, most of us tend to trivialize stress ("I'm sure it's *just* stress"), especially when dealing with the "small stuff." Finally, there is what I call the "principle of universality"—the idea that everyone experiences minor stresses every day, so they cannot be that important. Wrong!

Dr. Phillip J. Brantley at the Louisiana State University Medical Center has developed a daily stress inventory to assess the impact of minor stress events.[3] Read each of the fifty-eight items carefully and decide whether or not that event occurred *within the past twenty-four hours*. If it did, place an "X" in the space next to the item. To obtain your daily stress score, simply add up the total number of items you checked.

_____ 1. Performed poorly at task

_____ 2. Performed poorly due to others

_____ 3. Thought about unfinished work

_____ 4. Hurried to meet deadline

_____ 5. Interrupted during task/activity

_____ 6. Someone spoiled your completed task

_____ 7. Did something you are unskilled at

_____ 8. Unable to complete task

_____ 9. Was unorganized

_____ 10. Criticized or verbally attacked

_____ 11. Ignored by others

_____ 12. Spoke or performed in public

_____ 13. Dealt with rude waiter/waitress/salesperson

_____ 14. Interrupted while talking

_____ 15. Was forced to socialize

_____ 16. Someone broke a promise/appointment

_____ 17. Competed with someone

_____ 18. Was stared at

_____ 19. Did not hear from someone you expected to hear from

_____ 20. Experienced unwanted physical contact (crowded, pushed)

_____ 21. Was misunderstood

_____ 22. Was embarrassed

_____ 23. Had your sleep disturbed

_____ 24. Forgot something

_____ 25. Feared illness/pregnancy

_____ 26. Experienced illness/physical discomfort

_____ 27. Someone borrowed something without your permission

_____ 28. Your property was damaged

_____ 29. Had minor accident (broke something, tore clothing)

_____ 30. Thought about the future

_____ 31. Ran out of food/personal article

_____ 32. Argued with spouse/boyfriend/girlfriend

_____ 33. Argued with another person

_____ 34. Waited longer than you wanted

_____ 35. Interrupted while thinking/relaxing

_____ 36. Someone "cut" ahead of you in line

_____ 37. Performed poorly at sport/game

_____ 38. Did something that you did not want to do

_____ 39. Unable to complete all plans for today

_____ 40. Had car trouble

_____ 41. Had difficulty in traffic

_____ 42. Money problems

_____ 43. Store lacked a desired item

_____ 44. Misplaced something

_____ 45. Bad weather

_____ 46. Unexpected expenses (fines, traffic ticket, etc.)

_____ 47. Had confrontation with authority figure

_____ 48. Heard some bad news

_____ 49. Concerned over personal appearance

_____ 50. Exposed to feared situation or object

_____ 51. Exposed to upsetting TV show, movie, book

_____ 52. "Pet peeve" violated (someone fails to knock, etc.)

_____ 53. Failed to understand something

_____ 54. Worried about another's problems

_____ 55. Experienced narrow escape from danger

_____ 56. Stopped unwanted personal habit (overeating, smoking, nailbiting)

_____ 57. Had problems with kid(s)

_____ 58. Was late for work/appointment

_____ Total Daily Stress (Hassles) score

If you checked nine or fewer items, you are below average on daily stress. If you checked between ten and twenty-four items, you are within the average range. If you checked twenty-five to thirty-two items, you are above average on day-to-day stress. And if you had a score of thirty-three or more, you are a highly stressed individual! Those of you in the last two categories are, of course, more likely to experience toxic anger.

Dr. Brantley found that people tended to be consistent across time in the number of minor daily stresses they experienced. Therefore, the score you obtained today is probably a fairly good indicator of just how stressed you are on most days.

Alice's Daily Stress score was 9. It wasn't the "small stuff"—being late for an appointment or being interrupted during a task—that was making her angry. It was the accumulation of all the major events over the past year that finally caught up with her.

THE FOUR C'S: CUMULATIVE, CHRONIC, CATASTROPHIC, AND CONTROL

Certain types of stressful life events are more toxic than others. Some stresses build up over time (cumulative). Other stresses persist over time (chronic).[4] Others are considered traumatic because of the major impact they have on our lives (catastrophic). And, finally, there are stresses that seem beyond our capacity to control (control).

Alice, as we have just seen, suffered from *cumulative stress*. She had too many significant life changes occur in too short a time period. Alice had the "weight of the world" on her shoulders, and her angry outbursts were her way of saying GET OFF MY BACK!

David, the fifty-five-year-old "home tyrant" I described in Chapter 1, suffered from the *chronic stress* of endless back pain, which in his case had persisted for more than twenty years. Chronic stress leaves people like David feeling hopeless and defeated. Anger is David's way of saying I CAN'T STAND IT ANYMORE, GIVE ME A BREAK!

David is also an example of someone who is dealing with a stress that is beyond his *control*. The pain would not stop no matter what he or anyone else did. David took an endless supply of pain pills, went to physical therapy for years, and had surgery and countless injections, but his back continued to hurt. Anger was David's way of trying to reestablish some control in his life, if it only meant controlling the actions of others around him.

Finally, there are the *catastrophic* stresses. Judy is literally dragged down the driveway of the house she loves by a reassuring husband who tells her that she will be even happier when they settle in their new home in Texas. Martha watches the man she has been married to for forty years, "the love of my life," succumb slowly but surely to the ravages of Alzheimer's disease. Tony and his wife, Gwynn, try to deal with the tragic loss of their three-year-old daughter, who was killed by a drunk driver. Gene, an active man who has never been ill in his life, suffers a massive stroke three months after he turns fifty. Stephanie is the victim of a date rape. Are these people angry? YOU BET THEY ARE!

OUR CARRYING CAPACITY

Robert Ardrey, author of *The Social Contract*, a philosophical exploration of the origins of human aggression, used the term *carrying capacity* to describe the environmental role that space plays in promoting danger-ous aggression among lower animals.[5] The larger the space or the greater capacity animals have for separation, the less the incidence of violence. The smaller the space, the greater the incidence of violence.

The concept of carrying capacity can be applied to the human ner-vous system. In effect, some people have a greater capacity than others for carrying stress without showing signs of emotional strain. This stress tolerance is due in part to genetic differences in "stress reactivity" and in part to how people are raised.

There is no question that some people are more psychologically re-

I asked people who were close to me, "Couldn't you see that I was struggling? Couldn't you see that I needed help? Why didn't you intervene?"

They all said the same thing: "But, Doyle, you've always been such a strong person. Nothing ever rattled you. You could handle anything! You seemed to thrive on stress. You were the last person in the world I ever thought would have a breakdown."

silient and more stress resistant than others. Whatever your capacity for stress, however, you can always be overloaded. No human being has an infinite capacity for stress.

How do we know when we have exceeded our capacity for stress and have become *stress intolerant*? We look for signs of strain like these:

"Anything sets me off lately!"

"I can't seem to deal with anything anymore!"

"My fuse is getting shorter all the time!"

STRESS ADDICTION

Stress can be just as addictive as alcohol, nicotine, caffeine, and other stimulants. Like any potentially harmful substance, stress has an addictive quality: the adrenaline rush, the excitement of meeting a challenge, the "thrill of victory" that comes from winning a competition, or the sensation of being "on a high." As one woman put it, "stress is one way I know I'm alive!"

What if stress is necessary for you to feel alive? What if stress is the feeling you wake up to every morning in your life? What if you cannot remember the last time you felt truly relaxed? What if you have convinced yourself that you "thrive" on stress? Then you are hooked! You are the one who is putting yourself at risk for stress overload, not all those other people you blame. So why are you so angry at them?

Toxic anger is not always a sign of stress overload. It can also be a sign of withdrawal from chronic, addictive stress.

THE THREE R'S

1. *Relaxation* is the primary antidote to toxic stress. According to Herbert Benson, Harvard physician and noted stress researcher, each of us "possesses a natural and innate protective mechanism against 'overstress' . . . the Relaxation Response." Without relaxation, we cannot survive very well or for very long.

2. *Reserve* some time just for yourself each day. Become a priority in your own life. Do things that interest you and make you happy. Nurture yourself.

3. *Revisit* the quiet, peaceful moments from your past through visual imagery. Transport yourself through time and space to a "special" place free of the usual demands and pressures of everyday life: a secluded mountain cabin, a quiet deserted beach, that cozy French bistro.

EXERCISES

1. Dr. Benson suggests the following technique for eliciting the relaxation response:[6]
   a. Sit quietly in a comfortable position.
   b. Close your eyes.
   c. Deeply relax all your muscles, beginning at your feet and progressing up to your face. Keep them relaxed.
   d. Breathe through your nose. Become aware of your breathing. As

you breathe out, say the word *one* silently to yourself. For example, breathe in . . . out, "one"; in . . . out, "one"; and so on. Breathe easily and naturally.

e. Continue for ten or twenty minutes. You may open your eyes to check the time, but do not use an alarm. When you finish, sit quietly for several minutes, at first with your eyes closed and later with your eyes open. Do not stand up for a few minutes.

f. Do not worry about whether you are successful in achieving a deep level of relaxation. Maintain a passive attitude and permit relaxation to occur at its own pace. When distracting thoughts occur, try to ignore them by not dwelling on them, and return to repeating "one." With practice, the response should come with little effort. Practice the technique once or twice daily, but not within two hours after any meal, because the digestive processes seem to interfere with the elicitation of the relaxation response.

2. Treat yourself to a quiet lunch once a week and *don't be in a hurry to get back to the grind!*

3. Try not playing the radio while you are driving. Listen to (and enjoy) the silence.

4. Once every hour throughout the day, stop and take fifteen to twenty slow deep breaths. Breathe in through your nose, hold it for a second, and then breathe out through your mouth. It only takes ninety seconds to reestablish homeostasis!

5. Spend quality time with a pet. Watch how pets relax and then ask yourself, "Who's smarter, me or them?" Let them entertain you.

6. Read Linda and Richard Eyre's book: *Life Balance* and become skilled at "antiplanning," discovering serendipity, and using both sides of your brain.[7]

7. Find something to laugh at every day. The Bible says, "A merry heart doeth good like a medicine." Cut out humorous cartoons and share them with a friend.

8. Cultivate the fine art of "piddling." Leisurely spend an hour or two working in earnest on some trivial or trifling task.

> I have learned a lot about how to live a stress-free life from my basset hound, Arthur. It is quite simple. You rest throughout the day. You take long, unhurried walks. You engage in playful antics. You speak to your neighbors. You show your gratitude for every bone that is tossed your way. You "invite" everyone to love you. And you stay in close physical contact with human beings.
>
> It must work. Arthur rarely gets angry.

9. Take a hot shower or soak in a hot tub for ten minutes a day. It's great for lowering blood pressure and relieving muscle tension.

10. Have a good cry once in a while. Science has shown that stress chemicals are released through tears—emotional tears, not the ones that come from cutting onions. I truly believe that one reason women outlive men by an average of seven years is that they cry more.

11. Inoculate yourself against stress-induced anger. Each time you are hassled or faced with some major life stress, take a deep breath and repeat the following four self-instructional phrases to yourself:

    "Easy does it."

    "As long as I keep my cool, I'm in control of the situation."

    "My anger is a signal of what I need to do. It's time for problem solving."

    "I can handle this!"

    Repeat the phrases until you feel yourself calming down and only then decide what action you want to take.

12. Find a spiritual outlet. Medical research has shown repeatedly that individuals who regularly attend a religious service (doctrine or denomination doesn't matter) have less stress-related illness, such as heart attacks or high blood pressure, over a lifetime. There is something truly rejuvenating about connecting with one's "higher power."

Every time I start to get upset or angry about some little thing, I say to myself, "Hey, you had a lung removed and almost died when you were sixteen. You survived that! How difficult can this be?" And then, suddenly, things don't seem so bad.

♦ ♦ ♦

Does stress play a significant role in your toxic anger? If so, indicate it on the Toxic Anger Checklist found on page 50.

CHAPTER 10

THERE'S NO DEFENSE LIKE A GOOD OFFENSE

Nice guys finish last.

—Leo Durocher, baseball manager

Consider for a minute how differently three people handled the same frustrating situation: Each has just finished a long-awaited meal at a restaurant that has a reputation for fine food and impeccable service. Each had to wait for quite a while to be seated because of a mix-up with the reservations. The waiters were less than attentive throughout the evening, and the food was not up to expectations. And now it is time to pay the check.

Joanne, who is twenty-five and single, loudly demands to see the manager. "You people have some nerve," she protests, "expecting me to pay for a meal as bad as this! As for the waiter, I'd drop dead before I left him a tip! You'll never see me in here again!"

Mark, who is forty-two and married, thinks about saying something to the waiter about the poor service but decides otherwise. Mark doesn't like confrontations. Instead, he says to his wife, "I guess we just came on the wrong night." He leaves the usual gratuity even though he does not think he should, and when he is asked on the way out if he enjoyed his meal, he replies, "Yeah, it was fine."

Margaret, thirty-eight years old and recently divorced, takes the check to the cashier and calmly asks to speak to the manager. "I've heard really wonderful things about your restaurant," she begins, "but, quite frankly, our meal this evening was a big disappointment. We didn't see much of our waiter, and my food was almost cold when it finally arrived. I'm not one to complain, you understand, but I thought you might want some feedback about our impressions since this is our first time here. I'll be happy to pay the check, but I did not leave the usual gratuity. If I come again, I expect to have a more enjoyable time."

Joanne, Mark, and Margaret each has a distinct interactive style when it comes to handling situations that are potentially anger arousing. Joanne's style is aggressive. She actively tries to hurt, demean, and humiliate the other person. Her response is motivated by malevolent anger, the goal of which is revenge, and it is defined by a visible expression of emotion. Joanne wants the manager to know exactly how she feels about her meal. There is nothing subtle about an aggressive style!

Mark's style is quite the opposite, passive and submissive. He actively avoids unpleasantness, tension, or conflict. Mark is the type of person who often says things are fine when they are, in fact, not fine. Mark is afraid of what other people will think of him or what they might do if he becomes angry. His fear of embarrassment is much stronger than his anger. If Mark's anger is expressed at all it is covert or invisible. In this instance, he has little to say to his wife on the way home and is *dis*interested in doing anything after the meal. The positive mood he was in at the beginning of the evening has long since disappeared and is replaced by a mild sense of dysphoria ("I'm tired. Let's just go home") and pessimism ("I don't think there's anywhere in this town you can get a really good meal!"). Mark has temporarily buried his anger.

Margaret's style, on the other hand, is assertive. Margaret is standing up for her rights as a customer, but not at the expense of others. She expresses herself openly but without emotion, focusing on what she thinks about her meal rather than how she feels after having a bad experience. Like Joanne, she does not leave anything to the manager's imagination, but she is not seeking revenge, and she does not eliminate the possibility of returning for another meal. She leaves the door open for a return engagement, but with the clear expectation that she will be treated better the next time. Unlike Mark, she does not say the meal was fine when it clearly was not. She is honest and forthright, while at the same time calm and in control of her emotions. Her intent here is not to blame anyone but to assert her authority as a patron. Margaret knows full well that the power lies not in the hands of those who prepare and serve the food but in the hands of those who pay the bill.

Unlike Joanne, who is visibly upset, and Mark, who retreats into a tightly controlled world of silence and disinterest, Margaret leaves the restaurant feeling quite good about herself.

Because assertive people are neither victors nor victims, they do not need to be intensely angry or to stay angry for a long time. "Victors"—people who seek to even the score through an aggressive exchange—must be very angry to begin with to fuel their aggressive style, and their anger is slow to subside. Similarly, victims are typically very angry after a confrontation, often at themselves, because they lacked the courage to stand up for what they knew to be right, just, and reasonable. They settled for less!

THE AHA! FALLACY

One of my mentors, Dr. Charles Spielberger, coined the term *AHA! syndrome* to illustrate the assumed interconnections among the emotion of *Anger*, a *Hostile* attitude, and *Aggressive* behavior.[1] The basic assumption behind AHA! is that anger is always at the core of expressed hostility and aggression. When you see the attitude or behavior, you can automatically assume the emotion. If I yell at you ("You're an idiot! I hate you!") or if I act in a hostile manner ("Hurry up, I don't have all day!"), I must be angry.

What if I seldom or never act with hostility or aggression? What if I smile, say everything is "just fine," and quietly go about my business? Are you then to assume that I am not angry? If you do, you may be wrong.

To reiterate what I said earlier in the book, *most angry people do not "act out" their anger in any obvious hostile or aggressive way.* On the contrary, the vast majority—90 percent according to Dr. Averill[2]—"act in" their angry feelings by dealing with the world around them in a passive, submissive manner. Ironically, it is this "silent majority" who harbor the most anger but receive the least attention.

Many years ago, Dr. Paul Kirwin and I conducted a study of the relationship between "social constriction," or nonassertiveness, and the various aspects of the AHA! syndrome.[3] We found that our subjects' scores on the assertiveness scale correlated negatively with their tendencies toward both verbal aggressiveness ("When I get mad, I say nasty things") and physical assault ("When I really lose my temper, I am capable of slapping someone"). The more assertive the subject was, the less likely he or she was to act aggressively. However, to our surprise, the subjects' assertiveness scores were not at all related to their tendency to feel irritable or angry. We concluded that nonassertive people are just as likely to be angry in their day-to-day lives as assertive people, but they never let anyone know that they are angry. *What is being "constricted" is their behavior, not their emotion!*

Likewise, people who have an assertive interactive style are not as likely to suffer from toxic anger as nonassertive people. In fact, by behaving in an assertive manner, they deal more immediately and effectively with provocative situations and resolve the conflict before they become too angry. They also "let go" of their anger more easily because they express their opinions openly and honestly. Thus, assertive people are less likely to experience the toxic buildup of anger over time.

Holly was a "nice lady" who unfortunately was used to taking verbal abuse from her husband. They had been married for twelve years, and much of that time he had picked on her, criticized her, and found fault with everything she did. She always responded the same way, by apologizing for not being the perfect wife, vowing to do better, and then escaping into her inner world of tense silence, hopelessness, and depression.

Holly did not like being angry. She avoided it at all costs. Such feel-

My father was an angry, aggressive man. I knew by the time I was five years old that I didn't want to be like him. I didn't want people to hate me, to be afraid of me. So I became the exact opposite—quiet, passive, easygoing. I never raised my voice, never hit anyone, and for more than forty years rarely showed my anger. You never met a nicer guy!

But then somewhere in midlife, I found myself acting just like my father. Angry all the time, and aggressive too. You name it—I attacked it! From one extreme to the other. The scariest part of the experience was that I couldn't control it.

It took me quite a while to find the middle ground, but thank God I eventually did.

ings made her uncomfortable! But for some reason, tonight was different. Her husband was his typical abusive self. He had picked on her relentlessly all evening at a party in front of friends and again all the way home in the car. She could feel anger building inside her, but she had managed to smile and act as if things were fine. As soon as she walked through the front door of the house, she exploded! She hurled her handbag as hard as she could across the hardwood floors down the hallway toward the bedrooms. It crashed against the wall sending broken beads in all directions. At the same time, she screamed as angrily as she could at her husband, "Damn it! Leave me alone!" Both she and her husband were stunned by the intensity of her outburst. Holly felt both exhilarated and scared. She had never in her life acted this way.

SELF-ASSESSMENT

Do you suffer from toxic passivity? Do you stick up for your rights, or do you allow others to walk all over you? Do you say what you feel or what you think other people want you to say? Do you initiate relationships with attractive people, or do you shy away from them?

One way to gain insight into how assertive you are is to take the following self-report test of assertive behavior, developed by psychologist Spencer A. Rathus of St. John's University.[4] Indicate how well each item describes you by using the following code:

---

3 = very much like me   −1 = slightly unlike me

2 = rather like me   −2 = rather unlike me

1 = slightly like me   −3 = very much unlike me

_____ 1. Most people seem to be more aggressive and assertive than I am.

_____ 2. I have hesitated to make or accept dates because of "shyness."*

_____ 3. When the food served at a restaurant is not done to my satisfaction, I complain about it to the waiter or waitress.

_____ 4. I am careful to avoid hurting other people's feelings, even when I feel that I have been injured."

_____ 5. If a salesperson has gone to considerable trouble to show me merchandise that is not quite suitable, I have a difficult time saying "No."

_____ 6. When I am asked to do something, I insist upon knowing why.

_____ 7. There are times when I look for a good, vigorous argument.

_____ 8. I strive to get ahead as well as most people in my position.

_____ 9. To be honest, people often take advantage of me.*

_____ 10. I enjoy starting conversations with new acquaintances and strangers.

_____ 11. I often don't know what to say to attractive persons of the opposite sex.

_____ 12. I will hesitate to make phone calls to business establishments and institutions.

_____ 13. I would rather apply for a job or for admission to a college by writing letters than by going through with personal interviews.*

_____ 14. I find it embarrassing to return merchandise.*

_____ 15. If a close and respected relative were annoying me, I would smother my feelings rather than express my annoyance.*

_____ 16. I have avoided asking questions for fear of sounding stupid.*

_____ 17. During an argument I am sometimes afraid that I will get so upset that I will shake all over.*

_____ 18. If a famed and respected lecturer makes a comment which I think is incorrect, I will have the audience hear my point of view as well.

_____ 19. I avoid arguing with clerks and salespeople.*

_____ 20. When I have done something important or worthwhile, I manage to let others know about it.

_____ 21. I am open and frank about my feelings.

_____ 22. If someone has been spreading false and bad stories about me, I see him or her as soon as possible and "have a talk" about it.

_____ 23. I often have a hard time saying "No."*

_____ 24. I tend to bottle up my emotions rather than make a scene.*

_____ 25. I complain about poor service in a restaurant and elsewhere.

_____ 26. When I am given a compliment, I sometimes just don't know what to say.*

_____ 27. If a couple near me in a theater or a lecture were conversing rather loudly, I would ask them to be quiet or to take their conversation elsewhere.

_____ 28. Anyone attempting to push ahead of me in a line is in for a good battle.

_____ 29. I am quick to express an opinion.

_____ 30. There are times when I just can't say anything.*

For items followed by an asterisk (*), change the signs (+ to −; − to +). For example, if the response to an asterisked item is 3, place a minus sign (−) in front of the three. If the response to an asterisked item is − 1, change the minus sign to a plus sign (+). Then add up the scores for all 30 items to obtain your Total Assertiveness score: _____.

The following table shows how your score compares to the scores of other men and women.[5] For example, if you are a woman and your score is 23, it exceeds that of 75 percent of other women. If you are a

Women's Scores	Percentile	Men's Scores
55	99	65
48	97	54
45	95	48
37	90	40
31	85	33
26	80	30
23	75	26
19	70	24
17	65	19
14	60	17
11	55	15
8	50	11
6	45	8
2	40	6
−1	35	3
−4	30	1
−8	25	−3
−13	20	−7
−17	15	−11
−24	10	−15
−34	5	−24
−39	3	−30
−48	1	−41

SOURCE: J. Nevid and S. A. Rathus. "Multivariate and Normative Data Pertaining to the RAS with the College Population," *Behavior Therapy* 9 (1978): 675.

man with a score of 23, you fall somewhere between 65 and 75 percent of other men.

If you fall at or below the 30th percentile, you qualify as suffering from toxic passivity! You really need to be more assertive.

When it comes to assertiveness, I have undergone a radical change. Up until five years ago, I would have scored a −38 (2nd percentile). Today, I am a +58 (98th percentile). And, you know, I'm still a nice guy!

WHY PASSIVE?

Why do some people have a passive interactive style and others a more aggressive style? To a large degree, we are born with our "style"; it is part of our temperament. Some children are predisposed early in life to "move against the world"; they are considered ill-tempered. Others are predisposed to "move away from the world." They have a "shy" temperament.

One of the primary defining characteristics of shy youngsters is that they are incapable of spontaneous and uninhibited expression of emotion, including anger. You will note that I did not say incapable of feeling emotion, only of freely expressing it. Shy people, as a rule, tend to withdraw from a situation when frustrated and are reluctant to react when provoked by others. In other words, they lack assertiveness! Perhaps this is why they are also characterized by covert hostility and a distrustful attitude.

Not everyone with a passive interactional style is predisposed to act passively simply because of temperament. Many individuals adopt this style of dealing with life's problems as a result of adverse social experiences. In effect, they learn to be passive and submissive. They learn to be victims. They learn to keep their anger hidden.

Experiences involving physical, sexual, and emotional abuse, for example, are especially destructive and can lead to passivity. The important legacy of abuse is not the physical trauma that the abused person endures, but rather the "learned helplessness" mind-set, which suggests that nothing can be gained from standing up for one's rights or protecting oneself from harm. Learned helplessness involves the belief that you cannot control the outcome of any situation through your own actions. When feeling anger, the person who has learned to feel helpless thinks, "No, I shouldn't tell him how I felt. What good would it do? It won't change anything!"

EMOTIONAL SCAR TISSUE

In Chapter 2, I mentioned that one of the defining characteristics of toxic anger syndrome (TAS) is that it *most often reflects hidden, unconscious, pathological agendas* from a person's past that reemerge and find expression in anger. Although the anger may feel new, it is in all too many instances "old anger" that has come back to haunt the person. Why do I say this? Because when you examine why you got angry in a particular situation, you often see that it reflects the same old unresolved issues that have been evoking anger in you throughout much of your life.

Old anger in many ways is like the physical pain that results from scar tissue. Certain movements cause the scar tissue to impinge on a nerve, and the result is a flare-up of pain. Likewise, life events can impinge on hidden psychological agendas—emotional scar tissue—and cause a flare-up of emotion, be it sadness, fear, or toxic anger. The fact that these scars are emotional rather than physical makes them no less real or painful.

Alice's mood suddenly turned to rage when she heard her exboyfriend's voice on the answering machine. She did not even remember what he wanted. It didn't matter. Just hearing his voice again was enough to set her off. It was as if they were back together again, with him controlling her every move, criticizing everything she did, always having to have things his way. Just the sound of his voice brought back all those old, painful memories: those years of not standing up for herself, of passively going along with whatever he thought and whatever he wanted; all those times she heard herself say yes when she really wanted to say no; all those years of trying so hard not to let herself feel anger.

People with a passive interactive style tend to have a backlog of hurtful, unresolved emotional issues, specifically because they never act on their feelings. Drs. George Bach and Herb Goldberg, in their classic *Creative Aggression: The Art of Assertive Living,* refer to "hurt museums" as places where "nice guys" harbor secret resentments and hurtful experiences from the past.[6] They suggest conducting a "museum tour," listing all the hurts and grievances you find, and then sharing the list with others who are willing to listen actively.

QUIT INVITING PROVOCATION

Anger does not typically occur in a vacuum. More often than not, it is a by-product of social exchanges between human beings in the course of normal day-to-day life. People are most likely to feel anger in response to provocation, especially when that provocation is viewed as an attack on their "self."

What happens if a person chooses not to respond to a provocation and turns the other cheek or "lets things ride"? Won't that stop the provocation? Won't the other person back off and leave you alone? Actually not! In fact, *the less you react to provocation, the more provocation you invite,* meaning you will have more to be angry about in the future by not dealing with the provocation in the present.

♦ ♦ ♦

Twenty years ago, I was involved in a research study at the University of North Carolina at Chapel Hill that looked at the effects of different types of interpersonal "feedback" on aggressive behavior in college students.[7] Students were asked to set varying levels of electric shock for an opponent during a series of competitive exchanges both before and after overhearing that person respond in one of the following ways:

Passive feedback: The opponent said nothing about the shock levels set by the student in the first half of the experiment.

Aggressive feedback: The opponent angrily said, "That guy over there is really acting like a jerk! I mean, he's giving me some damned high shocks. What sort of creep is he anyway?"

Assertive feedback: The opponent was heard saying matter-of-factly, "That guy over there has been giving me some real high shocks." When told he could also set high shocks in return, he further replied, "I know that, but I don't want to do that."

It is interesting that when there was no feedback (the passive opponent), students set higher levels of shock in the second half of the experiment. They, in effect, became more aggressive, more provocative toward the other individual. When confronted with assertive feedback, however, students did just the opposite: They set lower levels of intended shock. In other words, they were less provoked. Students subjected to aggressive feedback returned the shock with the same intensity.

What conclusion can you draw from this? If you want others to treat you better, to annoy or frustrate you less, you have to assert yourself. Being passive is the worst response to a potentially anger-provoking situation. It only makes things worse. Ask any battered spouse if I'm not right.

THE THREE R'S

1. *Review* your rights as a human being:
    a. I have the right to be treated with respect by others.
    b. I have the right to express my feelings (including anger) and opinions.
    c. I have the right to say no without feeling guilty.
    d. I have the right to ask for what I want.
    e. I have the right to make my own mistakes.
    f. I have the right to pursue happiness.

I was so proud of myself. For the first time in forty-five years, I stood up to someone who was physically bigger than I was. I was walking on the track one afternoon, something I loved to do, and here he came. The big brute with the bandana around his head, going the opposite way around the track, challenging everyone who happened to be in the inside lane to get out of his way. And I always did. And I always got angry, more with myself, I think, than with him. But not today. Today, I just kept walking in that lane until he powered up to me, stopped abruptly, got red in the face, and then with a loud "huff" proceeded to move over and let me continue on. For once, he was angry, not me! The feeling of freedom I experienced at that moment was exhilarating. I felt like someone had lifted a thousand-pound boulder off my back. It was David and Goliath all over again, only without the slingshot.

2. *Remember* that being assertive is different from being aggressive. You are not being "ugly" or "mean" when you say no to unreasonable demands or when you express your own ideas, feelings, and opinions, even if they differ from those of others.

3. *Resist* the temptation to take the easy way out by responding passively and avoiding conflict at all costs.

EXERCISES

1. Learn to say "excuse you!" when rude, hurried people bump into you in public. Always saying "excuse me" implies you have done something wrong, even though you haven't.

2. Think of something you have a strong opinion about and write a letter to the editor of your local newspaper. Don't be afraid to say, "I am angry about. . . ."

3. When someone is provoking you, turn the tables by asking questions:

   PROVOCATION: "You're always late and I'm sick of it."

   RESPONSE: "Are you saying I've been late for every single appointment we've ever had or just this one?"

   PROVOCATION: "You could have done better on that test if you wanted to. You're just lazy!"

   RESPONSE: "Are you suggesting that I wasted my time in the library for three hours last night?"

4. When you are dealing with difficult people, always begin whatever you say with the word *I*. "I can understand how you feel. I feel just as angry as you do, but obviously for different reasons." "I understand that my car isn't fixed; what I can't understand is why you didn't let me know earlier in the day that I would need to make other arrangements." Starting a difficult conversation with the word *you* can cause the other person to adopt a defensive posture and invites a negative counterresponse.

5. Reduce your passivity from the bottom up. Try being assertive in situations that are "low risk." For example, would you be more comfortable being assertive toward someone you know or toward a stranger? Would it be easier for you to be assertive over the telephone or in writing than in a face-to-face encounter? Begin with some of the situations on the self-assessment scale that you indicated are "slightly unlike me" and progress to those that you see as "very much unlike me."

6. Write down three things that you have always wanted to do but have not for one reason or another:

   a. _____

   b. _____

   c. _____

   Select one and, as the saying goes, JUST DO IT!

7. Make assertiveness a "mindful" behavior. Keep a card in your purse or wallet to remind you *before you act* that in every situation you have three options: You may be (1) passive and run for cover, (2) assertive and stand your ground, or (3) aggressive and attack. Make the choice and the consequences yours!

♦ ♦ ♦

Does toxic passivity play a significant role in your anger? If so, indicate it on the Toxic Anger Checklist on page 50.

CHAPTER 11

DON'T FUEL THE FIRE

*Alcohol, in particular, is a terrible vehicle
for dissolving anger. It merely introduces
other problems. A rotted-out liver
and despoiled relationships do not make for happiness.*

—Dr. Melvyn Fein, *Integrated Anger Management*

TRANQUILIZING ANGER

Jennifer, who is twenty-six and pregnant, is an example of a "negative affect smoker," which is a smoker whose habit is typically reinforced by tension reduction (*affect* is another name for emotion). She currently smokes half a pack of cigarettes daily. Before becoming pregnant, she smoked three times that much. Jennifer has been smoking since age thirteen, or half her life! I asked her why she smoked, and she said, "At first, it was the cool thing to do. Then, it became a habit. And then I found it was a way to control my anger a little bit. I get mad. And instead of 'going off at somebody,' I just get a cigarette and walk off, calm down, and come back to the situation."

When things get really stressful, Jennifer, like many people, finds it easier to grab a pack of cigarettes and "tranquilize" herself than to deal with either the anger-provoking situation or the anger that follows. Smoking is also her way of denying that she is a very angry person. (She had a TA summary score of 4.) "Otherwise, I bottle my anger up so much that I just end up snapping one day and just going off. . . . Then I have this big blowout argument. For a while, I feel good. But then I do the same thing all over again." Smoking does not change anything: "It just gives me something to do until I calm down." She tried to quit smoking once, but failed.

Jennifer's story illustrates much of what is currently known about the link between nicotine and anger. The frequent experience of toxic anger is a risk factor influencing the onset of smoking in many adolescents.[1] Whether intentional or not, many smokers self-medicate with nicotine in an attempt to suppress anger as well as depression and anxiety.[2] It is true that the more nicotine a person ingests, the less likely she is to react aggressively when provoked.[3] Angry smokers are much more resistive than others to traditional smoking cessation programs. In one study done at the University of Montana, 61 percent of angry smokers either dropped out of treatment early or continued smoking after treatment was completed.[4] This result was in sharp contrast to the quit/failure rate of only 5 percent for the nonangry smokers who completed treatment.

Episodes of intense anger frequently cause ex-smokers to relapse.[5] In one nationwide study it was noted that anger was the second most often cited reason for relapse (26 percent); anxiety was the cause most frequently cited (42 percent), and depression was a close third (22 percent). Finally, the increase in irritability that many ex-smokers experience after they quit smoking appears to extend well beyond what could realistically be called the "withdrawal" phase.[6] In a study of 150 French ex-smokers, for instance, 94 percent of those who were smoke-free at the end of one year remained more irritable than when they were smoking. These individuals also reported significant increases in the consumption of caffeine and alcohol.

♦ ♦ ♦

The relationship between caffeine use and anger is much the same. Caffeine acts to suppress the expression of anger in situations in which people are provoked, causing them, in turn, to act less aggressively toward others. As with nicotine, there is a clear dose-response relationship between caffeine and anger. The more caffeine a person takes in, the less likely he or she is to experience or express hostility and anger.

In an experiment at the Louisiana State University Medical Center, for example, psychologist D. H. Cherek subjected a group of young men to repeated provocation after they consumed either caffeinated coffee, decaffeinated coffee, or a mixture of the two.[7] When the men drank regular coffee, they were 58 percent less aggressive after being provoked, compared to when they drank decaffeinated coffee. When they drank a "half and half" mixture, they were 35 percent less aggressive.

◆　◆　◆

What is true of nicotine and caffeine is even more true of alcohol. Alcohol, like the other two substances, is frequently used to numb a person's anger. Sheila, fifty-eight and a widow, is a prime example. Sheila was raised in an alcoholic family, and as a child she quickly learned that using alcohol was an acceptable way of suppressing feelings of anger and pain. "Looking back as far as I can, people in my family do one of two things when we're in over our heads, when we don't know how to deal with things, when we're doing what we're supposed to do but not surviving it very well. We either get 'mean' with it or we turn inward with it and get self-destructive. And I think I became self-destructive."

That is where the alcohol came in. Alcohol was Sheila's escape, her way of hiding from adversity. When I asked her about being angry early in her life, she recalled: "I'm not sure I can remember getting angry so much then. It came out more as self-pity, depression. I don't remember feeling like I had the right to get angry. I don't even remember feeling the anger or calling it that. I know I was—a lot—but I never actually felt it."

Sheila, in fact, was married and the mother of two adolescent boys before she ever recalled actually *feeling* angry, and that's the same night she first remembers getting drunk!

At first, the drinking, which escalated over the years, made her anger go away. "Sometimes it would be replaced with a euphoric feeling—mellow. Then, after a while, it didn't have any effect." It did keep her from

> My use of alcohol as a means of coping with life's problems started out slow but accelerated in my middle years. Life just became too complex, and I found myself feeling overwhelmed. It was more of a solvent than a solution—I know that now.

expressing her anger in some "outrageous" way, such as throwing things, cursing, or yelling. Instead, she found herself becoming chronically depressed.

It is interesting that Sheila described her mother as a "stopped alcoholic who was mean." Her mother was "one of the angriest people I've ever seen—and still is. Very angry! She could rant and rave for hours." To Sheila, *anger* and *mother* were synonymous, and she did not want to be like her mother. Not at all! So, no anger. Her mother had chosen anger over alcohol. Sheila chose alcohol over anger.

TODAY'S SOLUTION BECOMES TOMORROW'S PROBLEM

Stimulants such as nicotine, caffeine, and alcohol at best provide a means of temporary escape from the experience of extreme, incessant anger. At worst, these stimulants perpetuate and intensify toxic anger.

To begin with, stimulants speed up a person's nervous system, making that user more arousable, more excitable, and more emotionally reactive, not less. The mellow feeling that is often reported in the aftermath of substance use is, in fact, more illusory than real. As my colleagues and I discovered several years ago in a study of the effects of alcohol consumption on simulated driving, subjects experienced a "paradoxical increase" in anxiety when they drank.[8] *The more they drank, the more anxious they became!* In large part, their heightened anxiety reflected a marked increase in physiological tension—increased blood pressure, heart rate, respiration rate—identical to that reported with anger arousal.

Jennifer acknowledged that she used nicotine to calm herself when

I got to where I always had a drink or two when I first got home in the evening. I was tired, drained, and I wanted to relax so that I could have some quality time with my family. But instead, I got more and more irritable with each drink.

she felt angry, but she also admitted that smoking "keeps me right on the edge" emotionally. It is clear that when it comes to anger, her solution compounds her problem.

In addition, alcohol, even if consumed in small quantities, can cloud or exaggerate one's perceptions, causing an intoxicated person to misjudge the actions and intentions of others in a way that often leads to intense and accelerated anger.[9] What to a sober person may seem unintentional ("He couldn't help it"), to the intoxicated individual is purposeful ("She meant to hurt my feelings!"). When one is drinking, what would otherwise be felt as a petty annoyance is often upgraded to a feeling of full-blown anger.

Alcohol also has a disinhibitory effect on both emotions and behavior. Alcohol lowers the threshold for emotional experience, allowing people to feel things they would not or could not feel if they were sober. This was certainly true for Sheila, who never felt anger until she turned to alcohol as a way of coping with an unhappy, stressful life. Alcohol, as she put it, gave her the "right" to be angry!

Alcohol-induced mood changes can also affect one's mood when sober. Dr. Isabel Bimbaum and her colleagues at the University of California, Irvine, and the National Institute on Alcohol Abuse and Alcoholism in Bethesda, Maryland, found that women who reported drinking larger amounts of alcohol were more likely than women who drank less to experience anger when sober.[10] They were also more likely to be depressed in the aftermath of heavy drinking, which (as I discuss in Chapter 14) can also lead to increased anger. These investigators noted further that women who subsequently abstained from alcohol use experienced a significant decrease in anger (down 38 percent), whereas women who maintained their use of alcohol reported an increase (up 72 percent) in angry feelings over time.

It is also important to emphasize that one need not be considered an alcoholic to experience alcohol-induced mood changes in one's sober state. On the contrary, the women in Dr. Bimbaum's study were all classified as "social drinkers," and the amount of alcohol ingested was quite low by conventional standards.

A VICIOUS CYCLE

Many people are caught up in a vicious cycle of stimulant use and anger, which will eventually spiral out of control. Consider the fact that the rate of violence in persons with no history of substance abuse or other mental health disorders is only 2 percent, compared to 21 percent among persons with a history of substance use but no other mental health disorders.[11] It is irrelevant whether you first start using stimulants as a way of suppressing anger, begin experiencing steadily increasing anger as a by-product of stimulant overuse, or find that stimulant use and anger both relate to other personality or cultural factors. What matters is that you see how substance abuse and anger are linked and find a way to break out of the cycle.

WHY YOU HAVE A HANGOVER

The intensity of a hangover after an evening of drinking may to a large extent reflect how angry the person was while drinking. Professor Ernest Harburg of the University of Michigan, a longtime friend and colleague, found in a study of 1,266 current drinkers that "angry drinkers" had far more hangover symptoms—headaches, stomach discomfort, tremors, diarrhea, loss of appetite, anxiety—than did "nonangry drinkers" the morning after.[12] Women who became angry while drinking reported 32 percent more symptoms, and angry men reported 67 percent more. Only

I seldom use alcohol now, and it has made a world of difference in my mood swings. Don't get me wrong; I still enjoy a good drink. I just enjoy being free of anger and depression more. Anger management is about tough choices.

15 percent of the women studied fit the "angry drinker" profile, compared to 30 percent of the men. Whether they were normally considered heavy or light drinkers did not seem to make a difference.

THE THREE R'S

1. *Refrain* from using any and all mood-altering substances, including nicotine, caffeine, and alcohol. It is a small price to pay to free yourself from toxic anger.
2. *Reduce* your use of caffeine and alcohol to a safe, nontoxic level if you cannot quit altogether. You are probably "safe" with less than 300 mg of caffeine (equivalent of three six-ounce cups of brewed coffee) and four ounces or less of alcohol (equivalent of two drinks) per day. Bear in mind, however, that this may not apply to all individuals. It is said of the poet and writer Edgar Allen Poe, for example, that he could get drunk from a single glass of wine!
3. *Remember* that because certain stimulants are socially acceptable does not mean that they are without harmful consequences. It is important not to confuse what is legal with what is healthy.

EXERCISES

1. Inventory your use of stimulants over a one-week period. Record the time of day you consume caffeine (coffee, tea, chocolate, caffeinated soda, over-the-counter analgesics and cold remedies, weight-loss aids), cigarettes, or alcohol; the situation that you are in; and what you are thinking and feeling at the time. Do you see a pattern? Are you more likely to be angry, irritable, or annoyed just before you light up or take a drink?

2. If you are a moderate-to-heavy user of alcohol—more than four ounces of alcohol daily—consider seeking help through a local Alcoholics Anonymous group. That was the first step in Sheila's emotional recovery.

3. Ask your physician to prescribe a safe, nonaddictive tranquilizer if you are having difficulty dealing with stress or find yourself unusually angry. *These are also called antidepressants!*

Time of day	Consumed	Situation	Thinking	Feeling
10:00 A.M.	Cup of coffee	Alone	Can't find report I need	Irritated
1:12 P.M.	Cup of coffee and cigarette	Alone	Have to stay late tonight	Annoyed
3:45 P.M.	Cigarette	With friend	Will miss son's game	Annoyed
7:45 P.M.	Beer	With wife	It doesn't bother her if I miss the game	Angry
8:15 P.M.	Beer and cigarette	Alone	No one in this family cares about me	Angry

> **Friday night's the worst!** That's when the urge to drink is the strongest. The rest of the week I don't even think about it. A lot of it goes back to when I was a child growing up. My father did blue-collar work, and he got paid on Friday. He would always take the family out to eat, buy us whatever we wanted, and actually pay us some attention. The fact that he was drinking all the time didn't seem to matter—it was just part of those "good times" we were having.

4. If you smoke, start by eliminating your "favorite cigarette" of the day. Forty-four percent of smokers have the greatest trouble resisting the after-dinner cigarette. The next most precarious smoke is the first cigarette in the morning. If you can find a way to resist the urge to smoke at your favorite time of day, you are well on your way to becoming an ex-smoker. Do the same with caffeine and alcohol.

5. Stay socially connected. Married people are less likely to smoke, drink, and drink heavily than unmarried people. People who have friends are less likely to smoke. You are at your most vulnerable when you are isolated and alone!

6. Practice controlled, responsible drinking. Drink low-alcohol beer. Limit alcoholic drinks to a specific number. Alternate alcoholic and nonalcoholic beverages. Drink slower. Eat plenty of food before or while you are drinking.

7. Practice the stress-management exercises outlined in Chapter 9. Highly stressed people tend to smoke more, drink more alcohol, and consume more caffeine than less stressed people.

8. Find an alternative response when you get the urge to use an anger-enhancing substance. If you normally have the urge to smoke a cigarette first thing in the morning, take a walk instead, take a hot shower, or work the *New York Times* crossword puzzle. If you usually stop off some-

where for a drink after work, go to a gym and work out for forty-five minutes as an alternative.

9. Read Joan Mathews Larson's book *Seven Weeks to Sobriety* and learn about a proven nutritional approach to substance abuse and anger.[13]

♦ ♦ ♦

Does substance use play a significant role in your toxic anger? If so, indicate it on the Toxic Anger Checklist found on page 50.

CHAPTER 12

WALK IN THEIR SHOES

Jesus wept.
—John 11:35

If after reading this book you remember only one thing, remember this: *Empathy is the principal safeguard that we humans have against our own unbridled rage.* Without empathy, there is no such thing as civilized behavior. Without empathy, we are all potential barbarians!

EMPATHY NO. 1

To begin with, we need to distinguish between two similar but distinct interpersonal emotional reactions: sympathy and empathy. *Sympathy*, which I believe to be a far more common reaction, involves *feeling something for* another human being. If friends are excited about their daughter's upcoming marriage, I would certainly feel a sense of joy for them. Similarly, if I learn that a coworker has prostate cancer, I would feel concerned for that individual. *Empathy*, on the other hand, involves *sharing a feeling with* another person.

Jesus is said to have wept not because he had just learned of the death of his friend Lazarus, but because he shared the pain and sorrow he witnessed in the family and friends of this good man. It is said that "he groaned in the spirit, and was troubled," when Jesus saw them weeping. It may well be this abiding sense of empathy that sets great social reformers such as Jesus, Gandhi, Martin Luther King, Jr., and Mother Teresa apart from the rest of mankind.

American psychologist E. B. Tichener first applied the concept of empathy to the understanding of human emotion in 1909. *Empathy*, according to Tichener, was a purely physical reaction; he referred to it as "motor mimicry," during which one individual's nervous system imitates the emotional reaction of another individual. By mimicking, or imitating, another person's feelings, we share in their emotional experience. The feelings are transferred instantly and automatically from the object of one's empathy to oneself.

It is often difficult to distinguish on the surface between empathy and sympathy in that both incorporate an emotional reaction within the context of our day-to-day dealings with other people. Two things, however, permit an empathic reaction. First, there must be an emotional bond (or connection) between the parties involved. Ideally, mothers and infants respond empathically to one another, as do husbands and wives. Second, the empathic persons must have had a similar experience sometime in their past that they can reference when viewing another person's good fortune or plight. To experience empathy, at least one of these two factors must always be present. Otherwise, the best you can be is sympathetic.

Joan has a predictably empathic response every time she hears about someone losing a child. Whether she knows the person or not, she genuinely shares the pain of the loss. You can see it in her face amid the tears. Joan lost her first child in a miscarriage thirty years ago. Her husband was in Vietnam at the time, and there was no one to help her cope with this tragic loss. To this day, Joan reexperiences the loss of her unborn child every time she hears that anyone has lost a child.

EMPATHY NO. 2

Avery D. Weisman, professor emeritus of psychiatry at the Harvard Medical School, provides a second definition of empathy. In his book *The*

> I raised my hand to spank my son, and in that moment I saw the intense fear in his face that I had known far too often as a child. Those were my cowering eyes I was looking into, not his! All at once, the single, most important fear of my life was realized: I was on the verge of becoming an abusive father. It was as though he and I were one; the fear I felt "with" him in that split second overpowered my anger. I told him how sorry I was and that I loved him, and I have never raised my hand to him again. That was fourteen years ago and yet it seems like yesterday.

Coping Capacity, Weisman refers to empathy as "respect for another person's irrationality." Empathy is more than passive acceptance of a "different way of seeing things"; rather, it involves "an authentic desire to see the world through another person's eyes." By *desire*, Weisman means an active, purposeful, intentional effort to participate in another individual's intellectual and emotional life. The opposite of empathy, says Weisman, is *alienation*. The alienated person neither trusts nor respects the thoughts, feelings, or actions of others and feels as though "we are all strangers speaking an alien tongue."[1]

EMPATHY AND ANGER

The relationship between empathy and anger is complex. There are three ways in which the two appear to be linked. First, *a lack of empathy facilitates both the experience and the expression of anger*. Empathy is an emotional and intellectual "filter" through which we process the actions of others. As Weisman suggests, it signals that we trust and respect the "irrationality" of others even though we might not necessarily agree with or condone their behavior. The nonempathic parent angrily slaps a child who says no when told to do something. The nonempathic male college student angrily forces himself on his date after she says no to his sexual advances. By acting as a filter, empathy changes what might otherwise be a rageful response into something much more manageable, and it allows a person to bypass anger altogether, thereby dealing with daily conflicts in a more direct, rational, and problem-solving manner.

Second, *there is empathic anger.* If a person becomes angry when someone or something threatens another person or group with whom she has developed an emotional connection, she is exhibiting empathic anger. Examples include parents who become visibly angry when someone threatens their child, members of a minority group who become angry when they perceive the rights of other group members being egregiously violated, and dog or cat owners who become angry when someone attacks their beloved pet or other dogs or cats. Even though empathic anger can be viewed as a type of secondhand anger, it is certainly just as powerful and troublesome as the anger that arises out of direct provocation.

Third, *there is the anger we often experience when we search for empathic understanding from others and find none.* Most human beings, especially during times of personal crisis or peak stress, look to those closest to them for understanding. If we feel angry or have a hostile outlook, we expect them to be angry and hostile along with us. In short, we expect an empathic response, and we are apt to get even angrier and more hostile if they disappoint us.

I met Eddie in the waiting room, and I knew instantly he was upset. His face was as red as a beet, and I could see that he was close to tears. When I asked what was wrong, Eddie answered angrily, "Those bastards at the insurance company won't pay for a second opinion to see if I need surgery on my back!" When I reminded him that he already had seen eight different doctors for his back problem, he jumped to his feet and shouted, "I expected you to be on my side in this. I thought you cared about me. But you're no different than the rest—you don't give a damn about me!"

Eddie was wrong, of course, but at that moment his feelings were hurt. I had always been supportive of his efforts to overcome his back

> I confided to a friend about how angry I was that no one seemed to care that I was depressed for so long—not my family, not my friends, not even my mental health colleagues! She responded, "Doyle, you didn't let anyone know how bad you felt. You kept up the front as long as you could. Some of us would have shared your pain; you just didn't give us a chance."
>
> Once I realized she was right, I quit being so angry.

problems in the past, so he automatically assumed I would share his outrage at the insurance company. When I didn't, he redirected his toxic anger at me.

THE THREE R'S

1. *Review* your relationship with those closest to you. How "attuned" are you to what they are thinking and feeling?
2. *Remember* that empathy is not an all-or-nothing trait. Only a small segment of the population is absolutely incapable of empathy. Such individuals are called *sociopaths*.
3. *Realize* that empathy is a two-way street: The more you give, the more you receive in return.

EXERCISES

1. Read over some of the case examples provided in earlier chapters and decide if a lack of empathy played a role in each person's toxic anger. Recall Customer A and Customer B in the restaurant (Chapter 2). It's clear who was the more empathic.
2. Practice active listening. When someone you know is expressing emotion

including anger, do you interrupt and try to "fix" their feelings? Instead, just listen and try to feel "with" them for a change. Try being like my friend, Tom (p. 76).

3. Express your gratitude when someone responds to you in an empathic way. Empathy is a learned behavior and tends to repeat itself if rewarded.

4. Let people know how you feel. It is impossible to have empathy for someone who comes across to others as feeling*less*.

5. Set aside a designated time for sharing with others—spouse, children, friends, coworkers—on a regular basis, for example, weekly family meetings or thirty minutes of meaningful conversation with your spouse at the end of the day. Make sure everyone gets an opportunity to express him- or herself. Remember, this is a time for listening, not judging!

6. Try reversing roles with someone with whom you are angry. Challenge yourself to see things from his perspective. What is *he* feeling? What is *he* thinking? At the same time, let him put himself in your (angry) shoes. You can literally act your way into a more empathic state if you try.

7. Watch Stanley Kramer's Academy Award–winning film *Guess Who's Coming to Dinner* (Columbia Pictures, 1967). This is a poignant story about one man's struggle to find empathy in the midst of anger and racial intolerance. Think of this as a training film!

8. Get rid of roadblocks to empathy: pathological personality traits (Chapter 8), stress (Chapter 9), alcohol (Chapter 11), depression (Chapter 14), and the tendency to suppress emotion (see Chapter 16).

9. If you cannot get an empathic response for a specific problem—single parenthood, depression, chronic pain—from your usual sources of support (and that makes you angry), find a community support group (see Chapter 7) that will meet your needs. Empathic sharing is what support groups are all about.

◆ ◆ ◆

Are you lacking in empathy? If so, indicate this on the Toxic Anger Checklist found on page 50.

CHAPTER 13

EXORCISING

After the workout is over, the cup is empty.
—Greg

Some people are more reactive, more impulsive, more excitable, and more volatile than others. Greg and Anita are two such people. They both exude aggressive energy. Their speech is rapid, their posture tense, and their eyes blink excessively. When listening to others, they frequently interrupt and try to hurry the speaker along by uttering "uh huh, uh huh." Their tone of voice is emphatic. They constantly fidget. They seem always to be sucking in air as if they were out of breath. Their face, in the words of Dr. Meyer Friedman, often has "a look of anger under a thin veneer of civility."[1]

Anita and Greg share many of the biological tendencies that, as I suggested earlier, lead to heightened anger arousability and an increased potential for TAS. Greg scored a perfect +8 on the biological arousal scale (see pp. 44–45). Anita scored a +5. The only difference between them is that she tends to be more deliberate (to think before reacting) in her response to frustration, whereas he is extremely impulsive. Both Greg and Anita "exorcise"—exercise as a means of "purging" the buildup of nervous system excitation that would otherwise find its way into toxic anger.

Early in my academic career, I was invited to a two-week conference on a remote mountaintop in southern France. On the third afternoon, as we enjoyed the pastoral scenery sipping wine, my roommate, a psychologist from England, remarked that I always seemed to be tense. I said, "Oh, no, I'm quite relaxed, you know, thousands of miles away from the rat race of work, family, etc." I remember, he just shook his head and smiled.

GREG

Greg is thirty-six, married, and works for a sporting goods store. "I'm an impatient kind of guy," he says. "I expect things right away. If the light turns green and the person ahead of me doesn't start up immediately, I end up beeping the horn or saying a few words. If I'm in the middle of something and one of my children wants to throw a monkey wrench into that something, I have a tendency to react angrily. I internalize a lot of the reactivity that I might have to situations every day, and it tends to bottle-up inside of me. Anger, for me, is not a mental thing. I don't sit around thinking about being angry. My anger is reactive. And because I hold it in, it ends up filling me up, and then it has to spill out.

"Often it spills into physical things," he continues. "As a child, I would punch telephone poles, head-butt cars, wrestle rougher with my little brother than I should have—sometimes I hurt him! Even sometimes with my children, I have a tendency to be reactive when they don't do what I want them to or where they surprise me with something I'm not ready for. . . . My voice gets louder than it should. I say things I shouldn't say. I know I should count to ten when I feel myself getting angry. Too often, the physical side of my anger comes out.

"I try to work out three times a week, pretty regularly. I live a full life! If I don't release—from life—two, three, four times a week, I find it's easier for me to be reactive instead of thinking things out. When I exercise, I'm able to dump it off into the weights. I see anger as an adrenaline release, and I'd rather use it on an inanimate object than people. I'd rather just go in and breathe hard, yell and scream, grunt and groan, talk to myself, beat up on weights, or run myself into the ground with a workout.

"If I don't work out and release that energy, the cup starts to overflow—the voice gets a little louder, the grip on my child gets a little harder—and I know it's time to get back to the exercise. If I have an intense enough workout and physically tire myself out, it usually takes the edge off 99 percent of my problems. It's just my nature. I'm a 'get to it' kind of guy. I don't wait around for things to happen. If somebody asks me to do something, I move right to it—go, do, don't wait around!"

ANITA

Anita is twenty-seven, single, and a management trainee. "I'm a very focused, driven person," she says. "I like to have something to do at all times during the day. I like to schedule in my 'down' time. I don't like being still and nonactive. I like the sense—thrill—of accomplishment that comes with doing a lot. I find myself having a lot of energy. I'm easily excitable, more than most people I think, even about small things. Every stage of life, I've never been satisfied with doing the normal amount of things. I get tense and angry when things don't go quite as planned. I get irritated with people who display traits I have little tolerance for—laziness, incompetence, people who only pursue one thing at a time.

"I'm not as angry as I used to be. I was quicker to react. I could fly off the handle at any moment. Now, I don't get as immediately angry about anything. Now, I don't always feel the need to express my anger. I can be angry inside of myself, and I can find something constructive to do with it. I don't feel the need to hit something, yell, scream, or even cry. I don't feel the physical urge to do anything with the anger.

"I'll go pound it out on the treadmill or go run. I exercise every day, intensively, an hour and a half—running, aerobics, weights. Afterward,

I feel drained, but happy I took time for myself. When I don't make myself exercise, I'm tired, more irritable, and the smallest thing can turn into a large thing."

EXERCISE HAS A SPECIFIC EFFECT

Psychologist James Blumenthal and his colleagues at Duke University Medical School examined the potential benefits of physical exercise training in forty-six healthy, middle-aged Type A and B men and women.[2] They found that a program of ten weeks of supervised exercise, consisting of a combination of stretching exercises and continuous walking or jogging three times weekly, led to a significant reduction in the coronary risk profile (decreased systolic and diastolic blood pressure and increased high-density lipoprotein [HDL] cholesterol) for all participants. They went on to say, however, that only the Type A participants showed any evidence of a psychological benefit. They reported a 36 percent drop overall in Type A characteristics, such as impatience, overinvolvement with a job, hard-driving competitiveness. However, almost all of this change was specific to the hard-driving aspect of their Type A personality. Exercise apparently did not make them less impatient or less job-involved, but it did defuse their free-floating hostility and made them less likely to "goad, irritate, and infuriate" those around them. The Type B's, on the other hand, did not need to change!

FINDING TIME IN YOUR DAY

Modern-day living for many people means long, tension-filled days full of hassles. To prevent the buildup of toxic levels of tension, you may need to find time in the middle of your day for "exorcising." Waiting until the end of the day may be too late!

Ron, a thirty-eight-year-old draftsman, was in the midst of a midlife crisis. Although he was happy in his marriage, he felt his career was at a dead end. Younger coworkers were passing him by, and no one seemed

When I was at my angriest, walking was my salvation! I couldn't wait to get to the track each day so I could "walk down" some of the tension that was constantly building inside me. Afterward, it was as if a heavy weight had been lifted off me. I could go home then and be a fairly civil person.

to appreciate his contributions to the company. Ron hated going to work, and by midday he was seething with anger. He tried not to show his displeasure, but it was becoming more difficult to hide it all the time. His mood was depressed, and he was beginning to experience panic attacks—hyperventilation and chest pain—during the day. On two occasions, he left work abruptly without explanation. Ron was concerned that he might lose his job.

The solution was simple. Ron began going to a nearby gym during his lunch hour where he swam a hundred laps, relieving the tension and hostility that built up during the first half of his workday. This made it possible for him to get through the remainder of the day in a relatively calm state. Ron later confided in me that, while swimming, he visualized himself "angrily attacking his boss" or working in a new setting where he felt more appreciated. It wasn't long before Ron felt noticeably better; the panic attacks subsided, and his mood improved considerably.

I remember reading years ago that major companies in Japan—Sony, Toyota—had installed so-called tension control rooms for employees so they could periodically relieve their workplace frustrations by "beating the hell" out of plastic humanlike dolls with wooden bats. This was supposed to improve morale and in turn lead to a higher level of efficiency. It seemed to work. The same could be accomplished today by simply installing an exercise facility in the workplace—forget the dolls and bats!

A CAUTIONARY NOTE

Physical exercise, although potentially beneficial in preventing toxic anger, can also have its drawbacks, as in the case of Dorothy. Sixty-one years old when I first met her, Dorothy suffered from chronic depression and occasional panic attacks. Her emotional problems stemmed from a highly dysfunctional marriage, which left her with a tremendous amount of pent-up anger toward her husband. She felt unloved and virtually abandoned by this man, to whom she had been married for more than forty years, and she felt absolutely powerless to change the situation.

I had seen her only a few times when her husband called one morning to say that Dorothy was in the hospital. It seemed the two had gotten into a rather heated argument the day before just as he was about to leave town on business. He ended up storming out of the house in a rage, while she angrily climbed on her exercise bike (motivated by an "I'll show him!" attitude) and began pedaling away with a vengeance. Realizing that he had left the house without his briefcase, her husband returned home several minutes later only to find Dorothy lying on the floor crying and complaining of severe chest pain. She had literally pedaled herself into a heart attack! Her age, as well as the fact that she was overweight and had a history of high blood pressure, made intense exercise in this case a potentially self-destructive activity. Also, Dorothy used her exercise bike only sporadically, not as part of a program of routine exercise. Bear in mind that Greg and Anita were both much younger, in excellent physical health, and worked out regularly.

Recall George, the man whose wife called me because he was in the backyard screaming and beating a rake against a tree. Like Dorothy, he was at risk for a heart attack; he was overweight and had high blood pressure and a family history of heart disease. The major difference was that he was fifteen years younger than Dorothy and was used to moderately strenuous exercise.

THE OTHER SIDE OF THE COIN

Clearly, the emphasis up to this point has been on exercising as a means of getting rid of excess energy that can serve as a basis for excessive anger. But there also are people who find themselves lacking in sufficient energy to meet the demands of their day. *There is no excess here; there is an energy deficit, or shortfall!* When this occurs, the person experiences a predictable physiological change typically referred to as *fatigue* or *strain*. One notable consequence of strain is increased irritability.

Regular physical exercise has a positive effect not only on people's overall level of physical fitness—their strength, stamina, and flexibility—but also on their level of psychological fitness—their self-esteem, resiliency, and sense of mastery. The more physical resources one can bring to bear to cope with life's day-to-day challenges, the less strained one is apt to become. The less strain, the less likely one is to be irritable. It's as simple as that!

MANAGING THE EXTREMES

One important aspect of anger management has to do with effectively managing, or regulating, one's physical energy. Where you do not want to be, of course, is at the extremes, with too much or too little. Ironically, many people like Greg and Anita find themselves flip-flopping between these opposing states of exhilaration and exhaustion, both of which are highly conducive to anger. Exercise is simply a tool to help one maintain an *optimal energy balance* and thus optimal control of one's emotions.

THE THREE R'S

1. *Remember* not to have a competitive attitude when you are "exorcising." This is a time to calm down, to let go, and relax.
2. Find ways to *release* accumulating energy throughout the day.

An ounce of prevention along the way is better than a pound of cure later on.

3. *Reach out* to others who share your hard-driving tendencies and invite them to exercise with you. You are likely to stay with an exercise program longer if you have support rather than trying to go it alone.

EXERCISES

1. Before you embark on any type of exercise program, consult your physician. This is especially important if you are older than forty and/or have a history of heart disease.

2. Counteract those negative thoughts you may have about exercising:

Negative thought: _____ I can't afford it. _____

Positive thought: _____ Walking on the school track is free. _____

Negative thought: _____ I don't have enough time. _____

Positive thought: _____

Negative thought: _____

Positive thought: _____

Negative thought: _____

Positive thought: _____

3. Recreational sports such as tennis, golf, softball, or volleyball are a healthy way to unwind, if you remember not to get overly competitive. If you find yourself getting angry, it is time to quit!

4. The amount of time you spend "exorcising" depends on how tense or

angry you are at the moment. If you are only slightly irritated, a short walk or workout in the gym will probably suffice. If you find yourself ready to explode, you will want to spend more time purging yourself of these angry feelings.

5. The best results come when you exercise on a regular basis. Experts suggest exercising a minimum of three times a week.

◆ ◆ ◆

Are you suffering from toxic tension buildup or energy deficit? If so, indicate this on the Toxic Anger Checklist on page 50.

CHAPTER 14

AVOIDING THE BLACK HOLE

Most people would rather be angry
than terribly sad.

—John J. Ratey, M.D., and Catherine Johnson, Ph.D., *Shadow Syndromes*

Many people who suffer from TAS also suffer from depression. Estimates vary, but at least one out of every eight people, regardless of age, gender, and social class, experiences an episode of depression at some point. Roughly half of these individuals will suffer two such episodes, and a third will have three or more episodes. These estimates don't even include persons afflicted with milder forms of depression, known as *dysthymia*.

To see if you are one of the millions of people who suffer from either of these conditions, take a minute to complete the following self-assessment questionnaire:

SELF-ASSESSMENT FOR DEPRESSION*

Answer each of the following questions in terms of how you have generally felt during the past two weeks:

*Adapted from the Beck Depression Inventory.[1] The original form contains twenty-one items.

1. I feel sad or unhappy at times.

0	1	2
Not at all	Sometimes	Often

2. I don't enjoy things the way I used to.

0	1	2
Not at all	Sometimes	Often

3. I feel discouraged about the future.

0	1	2
Not at all	Sometimes	Often

4. I am less interested in other people than I used to be.

0	1	2
Not at all	Sometimes	Often

5. I cry for no apparent reason.

0	1	2
Not at all	Sometimes	Often

6. I wake up early and have trouble getting back to sleep.

0	1	2
Not at all	Sometimes	Often

7. I have lost my appetite.

0	1	2
Not at all	Sometimes	Often

8. I am more irritated than usual.

0	1	2
Not at all	Sometimes	Often

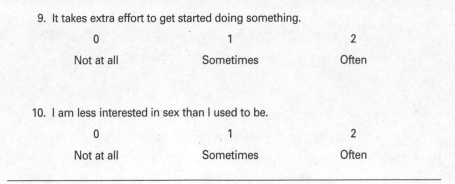

9. It takes extra effort to get started doing something.

0	1	2
Not at all	Sometimes	Often

10. I am less interested in sex than I used to be.

0	1	2
Not at all	Sometimes	Often

Now add up all your scores:_____ . If your total score is 4 or less, you are probably not depressed at this time. If your score is 5 or 6, you may be suffering from mild depression (dysthymia). If your score is between 7 and 10, you are most likely suffering from moderate depression. If your score is 11 or above, you may well be severely depressed.

Because some of the somatic symptoms of depression overlap with changes that result from a variety of chronic physical illnesses, such as hypothyroidism, chronic pain, or multiple sclerosis, your depression score may be inflated if you currently suffer from one of these illnesses.[2] In such cases, to obtain a more accurate estimate of whether you are depressed, do not include items 6, 7, 9, and 10 when you compute your depression score. Use the preceding guidelines to interpret the score you receive from the remaining six items.

MELANCHOLIA AND MALEVOLENCE

The intra- and interpersonal dynamics of depression and anger, for the most part, have to do with issues of *meaningful loss*. When we lose something of importance to which we are emotionally attached—a loved one, a job, material possessions, a pet, our health, freedom, a feeling of safety—depression is a natural emotional consequence. One dynamic behind this depressed state is *malevolent* anger (see Chapter 2), which

> Between 1989 and 1992, I never would have scored below 15 on this scale. For the past three years, I'm a perfect 0!

is either suppressed or acted out in some fashion. When depressed, we are filled with hate either consciously or unconsciously, because something that we love—something that is crucial to our sense of self—has been taken from us. When this malevolent anger is suppressed, we typically experience what is called a *retarded depression*, in which we lack the energy to act on our angry feelings. On the other hand, when the anger is acted out, as part of an *agitated depression*, we are prone to sudden emotional outbursts. The toxicity of a person's anger has more to do with the perceived magnitude of the loss in question than whether or not the anger is expressed. Other feelings that usually accompany depression include diminished self-worth, helplessness and hopelessness, loss of control, and isolation. However, the vast majority of the time, the melancholy experienced following a significant loss is short-lived. Only a minority of individuals stay trapped in a depressed state for long periods of time.

Les was one of those chronically depressed people.

LES'S STORY

Les is fifty-three years old, recently divorced, and an architect by trade. Up until ten years ago, he was a happy, carefree man who most would agree had a good life. He was well positioned financially and had a wide circle of friends, a loving wife, a nice home, and two children who adored him. Then without warning he was downsized out of a job he had worked at for nineteen years and left, for a time, unemployed and unable to provide for his family. The shock and hurt of being rejected by an employer to whom he had faithfully given 110 percent for all of his adult life was more than he could bear. Although on the surface he appeared unaffected by the loss and soon became reemployed, his behavior gradually began to change. He no longer showed any interest in socializing with friends. Nothing his family did pleased him anymore. He became obsessed with "everything being perfect." He would fuss because a book was left on a table, the top was left off a pen, or the pillows weren't right on the bed. At times he would vent his anger at his family, but mostly he withdrew into a stony silence.

A few years later, Les experienced yet another traumatic loss. His oldest brother, with whom he was very close, died suddenly of a massive heart attack. Then, only six months after his brother died, Les found out he had prostate cancer. He was losing everything in life that meant anything to him! He sank further into depression and his symptoms worsened. He never acted out his anger: He was not one to yell, scream, hit, or throw things. Instead, he would go for weeks without speaking to anyone in his family, retreating to the "safe haven" of his basement for hours every evening. He was a man literally filled with "frozen rage." He became cynical about the world in general and fatalistic about his own mortality. His wife tried for years to be supportive, but in the end she reluctantly filed for divorce. Les's unending anger and depression were simply too burdensome for her and the children.

Today, all alone, Les still maintains that he is not, and never was, depressed.

♦ ♦ ♦

Is Les's story unique? Unfortunately not. I am sorry to say I have listened to variations of this "angry tale of woe" hundreds of times, usually with the same tragic ending. The most damaging part, ironically, is never the loss that triggers the depression in the first place—the lost job, the child that dies, the amputated leg. Rather, it is the inevitable losses that follow as the person fails to recognize that he is suffering from toxic anger.

> I did everything I could to save my sister, but she died a tragic death at age forty-two. For four months, I felt nothing—no pain, no sadness. I worked seventy hours a week, drank a lot, and kept telling myself how lucky I was to be alive. Then one morning, without warning, I had a nervous breakdown.

ANOTHER VICIOUS CYCLE

Depression leads to anger, and anger leads to depression. It is often difficult to decide which comes first.

Depression, at least in some individuals, may be inextricably linked to anger through perceptual, chemical, and behavioral means. First, depression, especially when it is at a moderate-to-severe level, alters people's perceptions, for the most part leaving them with a cynical or paranoid outlook (see Chapter 8).[3] The depressed person begins to believe that everyone is taking advantage of him and not acting in his best interests. In more extreme cases, he believes that others are out to do him physical and/or emotional harm. Les, for example, genuinely believed that his family purposely failed to put things in their rightful place so that he would get upset. *The mind of a depressed person begins to play dangerous tricks!*

Second, depression, at any level, creates a chemical imbalance in the brain, which involves a deficit in two important neurotransmitters: *serotonin* and *epinephrine*. Neurotransmitters are chemicals that either block or facilitate the transmission of nerve impulses from one nerve cell to another. They are the basis for all communication within the nervous system, which, in turn, guides and directs all aspects of human behavior: thoughts, feelings, and actions. One of the primary functions of serotonin and epinephrine is to regulate emotional tone. When the levels are adequate, a person is apt to feel more upbeat or euphoric. Ironically, many of the factors or influences that lead to toxic anger seem momentarily to

I remember telling my therapist how ironic it was that I often felt much less depressed after one of my angry outbursts. A man of few words, he said simply, "Well, that's one way to treat depression, but I suppose there are better ways."

boost serotonin and epinephrine levels. Alcohol consumption, for example, leads to a release of serotonin in the brain. Stress increases epinephrine levels. Stimulants like nicotine and caffeine elevate one's mood through the same mechanism. Consequently, many depressed people in fact "self-medicate" by staying angry much of the time. Otherwise, they would feel the full brunt of their depressed mood. This may explain why, as Drs. John Ratey and Catherine Johnson suggest in their book *Shadow Syndromes*, violent men sometimes report feeling calmer when they are acting in an angry, abusive manner. For the same reason, some men and women seem addicted to rage. In these authors' words, "anger can bring sluggish areas in the brain up to speed."[4] *A depressed brain is a sluggish brain!*

Finally, as I discussed earlier (see Chapter 2), anger has certain positive functions that can counteract symptoms of depression by altering the depressed person's behavior. Anger energizes behavior and empowers an individual to act on the environment in ways that are self-serving and self-protective. In this way, anger serves as an antidote to feelings of lethargy and malaise, which lead to passivity and inaction. When angered, the depressed person often feels more like her former nondepressed self—more worthwhile. Why? Simple: She is behaving more like her "old" competent self. The problem, however, is that the mobilizing effects of anger are only temporary and last only as long as the anger does. As soon as the anger cools, the person reverts to her depressed self, that is, *until something or someone else makes her angry again!*

Anger, in turn, can also lead to depression in two ways; one involves chemical factors and the other, social factors. First, chronic anger can

> **Five cents a day is all that it costs me to take that little (anti-depressant) pill and keep my sanity.**

create a chemical imbalance resulting in depression. Just as alcohol is a stimulant in the short run but ultimately acts as a depressant on the nervous system, chronic stress, likewise, can alter brain chemistry, leading to a condition commonly referred to as *burnout*, of which depression is the primary emotional consequence. Second, people who suffer from toxic anger, whether they suppress or express it, effectively distance themselves from potentially supportive relationships with family, friends, and coworkers. No normal human being likes to be criticized, hollered at constantly, assaulted, or given the silent treatment. *If you want to chase people away, anger will do the job!* The ensuing lack of love and support provides a perfect breeding ground for depression. In addition, people who are prone to angry outbursts often feel guilty and ashamed after the fact, which leaves them feeling even more at a loss to engage the world in a way that ensures their own personal happiness.

THE THREE R'S

1. *Replenish* lost serotonin in healthy ways with the use of dietary supplements and antidepressant medication, with the help of a physician, of course.
2. *Resolve* the significant losses in your life rather than deny that they exist or run away from them. There's a saying I like: "You can run, but you cannot hide!" That applies here.
3. *Refer* yourself (or have a physician refer you) for professional mental health treatment if you think you are suffering from depression. Ask yourself when you were last "in a really positive mood" for any length of time. If you cannot remember when that

> **Psychotherapy is the reason I'm alive today. Thank God, I got sick and got help before managed care came along.**

was or it has been two months or longer, it may be time to seek help.

EXERCISES

1. Read the novelist William Styron's personal account of depression, *Darkness Visible: A Memoir of Madness*.[5] It is both informative and inspiring!

2. Have someone you trust (and who knows you) fill out the depression questionnaire *for you*, and see if your subjective view of your mood is accurate. Discuss any differences that arise.

3. Abstain from alcohol (see Chapter 11); it only makes depressed people more depressed.

4. Exercise regularly (see Chapter 13). It is a proven scientific fact that, at least for people suffering from mild depression, exercise can do as much to improve your mood as conventional psychotherapy.

5. Check your local newspaper or call your local mental health association to see if there is a depression support group in your community. If so, go to one of the meetings. If not, think about starting one yourself.

6. Depression is, by definition, a self-absorbing illness. Find something other than yourself to be concerned about. Sometimes, the more you invest in "worthy" causes, the less unworthy you feel!

7. Limit the use of tranquilizers. Depression and irritability are often side effects of these types of drugs.

8. Talking is still the best medicine for depression. Find someone who is an

empathic listener and share your feelings. Do not make the mistake Les did and end up losing everything!

♦ ♦ ♦

Does depression play a significant role in your toxic anger? If so, indicate it on the Toxic Anger Checklist on page 50.

CHAPTER 15

IF IT'S BROKE, FIX IT

Don't get mad . . . get even!

—Alan Abel, satirist

Apart from being an emotion, anger is also a means of coping with life's frustrations. Dr. Avery Weisman, author of *The Coping Capacity,* defines coping as any "strategic effort to master a problem, overcome an obstacle, or answer a question . . . that impedes our progress" on the road to survival.[1] For most people, at one time or another, anger does just that—it answers someone's question, it solves a problem, it seemingly brings order into chaos. But what if anger is the only way a person has to cope with the stresses of everyday life? What if anger is her first, last, and only option when it comes to coping? Then she suffers from TAS! Anger, in effect, only becomes maladaptive (toxic) when it is used as a coping technique in this indiscriminate and excessive fashion.

For the most part, anger is a defensive coping strategy. That is, it involves an attempt on the part of an individual to "fend off" problems rather than attempt problem-solving. A forty-three-year-old man spends years angrily complaining about the fact that he was injured on the job and can no longer work *instead of* finding a new way to lead a useful and meaningful life. A young husband and wife bitterly argue over unpaid bills month after month *instead of* planning a family budget that fits their joint income. An angry minister denounces his congregation every Sun-

> **I wasted a lot of time being angry instead of doing what I needed to do to gain control of my life. Once I started taking charge of things, there was a lot less to be angry about.**

day for their unwillingness to tithe *instead of* addressing the fact that membership is declining because of his failure to meet their spiritual needs. A nurse angrily recounts the frustration of working for an inept supervisor *instead of* looking for another job. It is simply easier to avoid problems by being angry than to fix them!

◆ ◆ ◆

Anger, according to Stanford University psychologist Rudolph H. Moos, is an example of *emotion-focused* coping.[2] This type of coping is aimed primarily at maintaining or restoring one's emotional equilibrium. Recall Rachel, the forty-two-year-old mother who used anger as a defense against the pain of past physical, emotional, and sexual abuse. Or John, the ex-Marine who used anger as a way of coping with the pain of social rejection. Or Carl, age twenty-eight, who used anger to cope with his feeling of utter helplessness when his children accidently unplugged the freezer and he lost $600 worth of meat. Alice used anger as a way to relieve burdensome levels of stress, and Les became angry rather than deal with the ever-changing world over which he had less control.

People who suffer from TAS, in essence, are constantly substituting one negative emotion—anger—for another—fear, sadness, helplessness. At the time, this coping method may seem effective because anger leaves one feeling momentarily empowered. In the long run it has more cost than benefit, given the potential medical, legal, and social consequences of toxic anger.

Other forms of emotion-focused coping include trying to reduce physical and psychological tension by eating more, smoking more, or using alcohol and caffeine. Sound familiar?

◆ ◆ ◆

Adaptive coping is not defined by one particular coping strategy. Rather, it involves the balanced use of a range of coping strategies, all of which can be effective, according to Weisman, "given the right time, place, problem, and person to carry them out." He offers the following fifteen coping strategies:[3]

1. Seek information and guidance.
2. Share concern and seek consolation.
3. Laugh it off—change the emotional tone.
4. Put it out of your mind.
5. Keep busy and distract yourself.
6. Confront the person, problem, or situation.
7. Redefine the problem—try to see things differently.
8. Resign yourself to that which can't be changed.
9. Just act—do something, anything, perhaps exceeding good judgment.
10. Consider the alternatives and examine the consequences.
11. Escape—get away from it all.
12. Conform—do what is expected.
13. Blame or shame—assign fault for a misfortune to someone other than yourself.
14. Give vent—seek emotional release.
15. Deny reality as much as possible.

Which of these coping techniques do you use a lot? Are there strategies that you rarely or never use? Can you confront a problem without being angry? Do you have to get angry in order to escape a problematic situation? Do you ever vent emotions other than anger? Can you turn anger into amusement? The answers to these questions may determine whether or not you suffer from TAS.

When people cope with a problem by becoming angry, this choice is not always conscious. In fact, most of the time, we react out of habit. We learn how to cope with problems early in life and then we automatically

> **These days I'm amazed at the things I can laugh at that used to make me boiling mad.**

and unconsciously repeat these "lessons" throughout our lifetime. *Fortunately, habits can be replaced.*

◆ ◆ ◆

Sometimes anger is not a way of coping but an existential state—*a state of being as opposed to doing.* Coping implies a sense of doing, as in removing an obstacle, seeking revenge, or solving a problem. Existential anger, on the other hand, is anger merely for the sake of being angry. It is not a means toward an end but an end in itself. People with existential anger choose to be angry instead of dealing with life's problems and expend much of their energy being angry, which leaves them less energy for effectively dealing with their many problems. To paraphrase Dr. Weisman, by failing to cope they impede their own progress in life.

THE THREE R'S

1. *Retaliate* without anger. This is the essence of Alan Abel's humorous little book *Don't Get Mad . . . Get Even!*[4] Example: If you have poor service in a restaurant, leave a tip—a card that says, "You were conspicuous by your absence!"
2. *Replace* ineffective coping techniques—those that cost more than they benefit—with those that are more effective.
3. Become a *role model* for adaptive coping at home, at work, and in your community. You may be surprised how quickly others follow your lead.

> **How did people in my family cope with problems? They got angry.**

EXERCISE

Keep a coping diary for a week and see how well you cope with life's many frustrations. At the end of the day, take a few minutes and recount the events that were most difficult or problematic. Write each down and then record a number indicating which of Dr. Weisman's fifteen coping strategies you used at the time. At the end of the week, look at the numbers and see if a pattern emerges. Don't be surprised if you have a lot of No. 14s!

Date	Problem	Coping strategy
1/4/97	Criticized by coworker	No. 6—confronted him
	Stuck in traffic	No. 8—resigned self

♦ ♦ ♦

Is anger your primary way of coping with life's frustrations, obstacles, and challenges? If so, indicate it on the Toxic Anger Checklist found on page 50.

CHAPTER 16

READ MY LIPS

Tell us thy troubles, and speak freely.
A flow of words doth ever ease
the heart of sorrows

—Howard Pyle, *The Merry Adventures of Robin Hood*

In the 1957 movie *Kiss Them for Me*, a somewhat stressed but always droll Cary Grant explains to his girlfriend why he has just punched another man in the mouth: "It saves a lot of conversation." Although comedic in tone, Grant's quip captures an essential point about toxic anger: *It can be an emotional shortcut to a well of unspoken hurts and grievances that build up in a person over time.* These shortcuts sometimes prove costly, both socially and medically, whereas the right kind of communication can have long-term health and lifestyle benefits.

I CONFESS . . .

Psychologist James W. Pennebaker at the University of Texas at Austin has spent twenty years studying the impact of self-disclosure, or confession in lay terms, on the physical and psychological health of human beings.[1] Thus far he has found the average person much more willing to talk about disturbing and traumatic issues with strangers in a laboratory setting than with people close to him or her. Pennebaker concludes that people seem to have an underlying need to confess. Inhibition is a source of physical and psychological tension for most of them.

Pennebaker also found that once people are given the opportunity to talk about their feelings concerning life stressors—relationship problems, illness, death of parents, and so on—it is difficult to stop them from venting their anger. Sharing some of the more profound stressors, in fact, easily elicited visible expressions of rage, such as wavering voices and crying.[2] His subjects, who ranged from college students to Holocaust survivors, had a backlog of suppressed emotions, such as hurt and sadness, that were not being adequately communicated.

My experience working with people suffering from chronic pain is very similar. I ask these patients to relate their "pain stories"—everything of significance that has happened in their lives since the onset of pain—in their own words and without interruption when I first meet them. When they finish, many are in tears and some are so angry they literally cannot sit still, pacing around my office like a wild animal! With a simple request to "tell me how things have been since you got hurt," I invite an outpouring of intense emotion—fear, sadness, rage—that is impressive to behold. A colleague once remarked that he thought this was why I was so successful in gaining the trust and confidence of such difficult patients: I was willing to listen to their stories when no one else would.

Self-disclosure seems particularly helpful in preventing negative emotions from escalating over time and interfering with future successes and general happiness in life. This was illustrated in a study by Dr. Pennebaker and his colleagues of fifty men who were suddenly downsized out of jobs. The researchers had twenty-five men write down their "deepest thoughts and feelings about being laid off" for thirty minutes each day for a week. The other twenty-five (control group) were not asked to write down anything. The men who wrote expressing the "humiliation and outrage" of losing their jobs said they felt much better after writing each day. More important, however, is the finding that those who "confessed" in writing were three to five times more likely to be reem-

> My mother was a hairdresser, and I'm a psychotherapist. Between us, we've heard a lot of confessions!

ployed several months later than were those who did not. Dr. Pennebaker surmised that these men were probably less defensive and hostile when they went on job interviews and thus came across as "more promising candidates." I suspect that their openness in coming to terms with the anger after losing their jobs also engendered a more empathic response (see Chapter 12) from prospective employers.

Do you find yourself wondering how different the life of Les, the depressed architect, would be today if he had "confessed" how hurt he was about being laid off, how lost he felt after his brother died, and how afraid he was that he might die from cancer? He might still be happily married, enjoying a rich family and social life, instead of finding himself all alone, angry, and depressed.

I'M A PRIVATE PERSON

Many people are open when it comes to expressing their emotions. You never have to guess if they are upset or angry; they tell you! Others, like Les, seem to lack this capacity for self-disclosure. They are reluctant to "go public" with their innermost thoughts and feelings, even to those closest to them. Minor irritants, fears, and petty grievances are "stored up" until they collectively reach a point of toxic anger, which, as I've discussed (see Chapter 2), is seldom expressed in an overtly aggressive manner. What happens instead is illustrated by a five-year study of blood pressure in ten thousand Israeli civil service employees, conducted by epidemiologist Harold Kahn at the National Institutes of Health.[3] Kahn and his colleagues found that men whose blood pressure was initially normal were much more likely to suffer from high blood pressure (160+ mm Hg systolic, 95+ mm Hg diastolic) five years later if (1) they tended to brood or restrain retaliation when their feelings were hurt by someone at work or (2) they experienced marital conflict that they usually or always kept to themselves. Men who did not exhibit these suppressive tendencies were less likely to show a rise in blood pressure during the five-year period. The "health risk" associated with inhibiting one's emotions in this instance was equal to that of smoking cigarettes or being obese, which have long been known to increase blood pressure.

The basis for this "private" personality is to a large extent—50 to 60 percent—genetic. In essence, humans are predisposed to be either private or public persons much the same way we inherit eye and hair color, height, and body composition. Life circumstances, on the other hand, can modify these biological tendencies, making them more or less a part of our emerging personality.

How do you know if you are a private or inhibited personality? Refer to Chapter 10. If you scored at or below the 30th percentile on Rathus's assertiveness inventory, you most likely have a private personality.

A WORD IS WORTH A THOUSAND PICTURES

The next best thing to verbalizing negative emotions is writing them down. Dr. Pennebaker and his colleagues have repeatedly found that keeping a daily journal of significant thoughts and feelings can improve immune function, cut down on the number of visits to a physician, cause a drop in days missed from work, and lead to improved grades and better employment. The method is simple. Write continuously without concern for spelling or grammar. Focus on negative rather than positive emotions. Use words such as *understand*, *realize*, and *because* more and more as you tell your emotional story. Most important, realize that it is the act of writing itself that is therapeutic, not the end result.

When I conduct anger management groups, I always devote one session to having participants "write out" any negative feelings they have about present or past life situations. It is interesting to observe how slowly they start out, as if they feel nothing, but how quickly the mo-

PRIVATE PERSONALITY

♦ You are shy around members of the opposite sex.

♦ You don't complain when you are dissatisfied about something.

♦ You have difficulty saying no when others try to take advantage of you.

♦ You hate to argue even when you feel strongly about something.

♦ You become anxious in social situations.

♦ You are overly concerned about what others think.

♦ You are easily embarrassed.

♦ You often find yourself speechless.

mentum picks up to the point that all participants are writing with a "vengeance" at the end. Most report being genuinely surprised at how much emotional "junk" they have bottled-up, of which they are unaware. As exercises go, this one is a real attention-getter!

A similar technique that I often use in psychotherapy is to have clients write an uncensored letter to someone for whom they have unresolved, angry feelings: an abusive parent or spouse, drunk driver, rapist. Subsequently, I ask the client to read the letter aloud. *He has to say the words for the technique to work*. The emotional response is both immediate and dramatic! (We never mail those letters, by the way.)

TONE IT DOWN

Effectively communicating your feelings for the benefit of better mental and physical health also depends on *how you say* what is on your mind. Psychologist Aron Wolfe Siegman at the University of Maryland Baltimore County, for example, found that people who have a *fast-loud* style of speaking when provoked rate themselves as much angrier (a 50 to 60 percent difference) than people who speak in a *slow-soft* voice. "As people get angry," says Siegman, "they experience an increase in cardiovascular

> **I wish I had understood the importance of "toning it down"
> when I got angry at my children. They might have actually listened
> to more of what I had to say, which really was for their own good,
> instead of "tuning me out."**

reactions, accelerate their speech, and raise their voices."[4] This increase in angry "tone" further heightens their physiological arousal and feelings of anger, and so on, in effect, setting up a vicious cycle between physiology and behavior. All this, of course, is made worse if the person on the receiving end of your anger reacts in a similar manner, which only adds to the acceleration effect. This is yet another instance in which "two wrongs definitely do not make a right!"

THE THREE R'S

1. *Ratchet* down the intensity of your anger by communicating your grievances in a slow-soft voice. People are much more likely to "get the message" that way.

2. *Register* your complaints about daily life in a personal journal. An exercise can be simple, cheap, yet highly effective.

3. Be *reflective* in communicating your feelings. Question why you feel the way you do. Do you become angry in situations in which other people do not? If so, why?

EXERCISES

1. Eliminate all aggressive, inflammatory language (SOB, jerk, idiot, fool) when you communicate your feelings to others. All these words do is put the other person on the defensive!

2. Take an acting class. You may be surprised at how the communication skills you learn on stage carry over into your private life.

3. Tape-record yourself the next time you get angry. Are you speaking too fast? Too loud? If so, try deescalating your anger by saying the same words but at a slower pace and with a softer tone.

4. When your anger begins to escalate, try the breathe in, breathe out technique (see Chapter 9). By controlling your level of physiological arousal, you automatically control the volume of anger.

5. Do you have a confidant—someone with whom you can share your innermost thoughts and feelings freely, without fear of judgment? If so, how much contact do you have with him or her? Remember, a resource is only a resource to the extent that you use it.

◆ ◆ ◆

Are you suffering from toxic inhibition of emotion? Are you too vocal when you are angry? If so, indicate this on the Toxic Anger Checklist on page 50.

CHAPTER 17

TAKING CARE OF NUMBER 1

Why are you in my business?
—A caustic friend

I recently attended a writers' conference where one of the authors proudly exclaimed, "I just completed my latest book on mental health, and believe it or not, I made it all the way through without once using the word *codependent!*" In jest, he was addressing the gross overuse of the term *codependency*, which has been offered as an explanation for most of the emotional ills that affect modern-day people. However, as applied to toxic anger, codependency is far too central to the understanding of "why people get so angry" to be ignored. Popular writer Melanie Beattie in her best-selling book *Codependent No More* characterizes co-dependent people as those who[1]

+ find themselves saying yes when they mean no
+ overcommit themselves
+ feel harried and pressured
+ take things personally
+ feel like victims
+ expect themselves to do everything perfectly
+ push their thoughts and feelings out of their awareness because of fear or guilt

+ abandon their routine because they are so upset about somebody or something
+ wonder why they never have any energy
+ don't say what they mean
+ eliminate the word *no* from their vocabulary
+ have a difficult time asserting their rights
+ have a difficult time expressing their emotions honestly, openly, and appropriately
+ don't trust other people
+ feel safer with their anger than with hurt feelings
+ find it difficult to be close to people
+ find it difficult to have fun and be spontaneous
+ feel depressed
+ become addicted to alcohol and other drugs

Does the list sound familiar? These are the same characteristics that, as you know from reading the preceding chapters, lead to toxic anger: cynicism and compulsivity, stress, lack of assertiveness, substance abuse, feelings of alienation, energy deficit, depression, emotion-focused coping, and poor communication.

Codependency is defined as *a habitual, compulsive need to control the behavior of others as a means of feeling satisfied with and about oneself.* Beattie suggests that codependency inevitably leads to both an "abandonment of self" and an "abundance of anger." The abandonment of self comes from the fact that codependent people devote little, if any, time and energy to their own need satisfaction, focusing instead on the needs of significant others—spouse, child, relative, client, friend—who assume number one priority in their lives. The message of codependency is clear: "My emotional life is in *your* hands. *You* can make me happy or not. The choice is entirely *yours*." Unfortunately, all too often, the codependent person ends up hurt and disappointed by the actions of the very people on whom they depend, and therein lies the source of much of their anger.

The following exchange, with one of my long-term therapy clients,

> I was forever shouting, "Get off my back! Give me a break!" to those people I felt obliged to take care of. But they weren't the problem. I was. I was the monkey on my back, not them.

illustrates the link between codependency and toxic anger. Richard is a forty-seven-year-old attorney who by all outward appearances is a happily married man. He has two children, both teenagers, and an above-average income. He enjoys good physical health, attends church regularly, and has a close circle of friends. Richard should be happy, but he's not. Far from it, he suffers recurrent bouts of depression and he has been known to abuse alcohol.

RICHARD: My wife reminded me last night of something we had to do this coming weekend, and I really got mad. When am I going to have some time for myself? It's always gotta be something she wants, the kids need . . .

DR. GENTRY: Excuse me, but what do you want to do Saturday?

RICHARD: [Angrily] I just told you, I have to do these things with my family . . .

DR. GENTRY: I heard what you said. But I asked you what *you* wanted to do next Saturday. I didn't ask what your wife wants you to do, what the kids need. What do *you* want to do on that day?

RICHARD: [Pause] I don't know what the hell I want to do. But I do know I'm getting angry with this conversation.

DR. GENTRY: I can see by the muscles in your neck that you're getting angry. And I can hear it in the tone of your voice. Do you know why you're angry at me?

RICHARD: Because I don't have an answer for you. And I get angry when I can't answer a question.

DR. GENTRY: I'm sure you do.

RICHARD: So where do we go from here?

DR. GENTRY: Well, try to look at it from my perspective. You are a very intelligent, successful man. And you apparently have managed to satisfy a lot of other people's needs these past forty years—your parents, wife, children, in-laws, clients, friends, etc. Yet you can't tell me how you want to spend one day of your life without bringing these other people into the picture. Doesn't that strike you as odd?

RICHARD: [Obviously sad] I suppose.

Richard was so accustomed to anticipating, and then satisfying, other people's needs, while at the same time neglecting his own, that he could no longer think, feel, or act except in the larger context of these other people. I wasn't simply asking Richard what he wanted to do with one day of his life; I was putting a much more basic question to him: "Who are you and what do you want to do with your life?" He became angry because I asked him to look into this "mirror of life" and tell me what he saw, and he saw nothing apart from being someone's husband or someone's parent. A second dynamic underlying his intense anger was the fact that Richard felt powerless to change. He felt trapped and miserable. He saw himself as a victim, and for the first time in his life, *he appreciated the fact that he was a victim of his own making!*

Sadly, Richard is but one of millions!

♦ ♦ ♦

Fortunately, there is no genetic basis for codependency, unlike empathy and depression. Codependency is a learned style of relating to others—a bad habit—nothing more. Like all learned behaviors, it can be *un*learned. That's the good news!

THE WOMAN WHO TURNED HER LIFE AROUND

Sally, a sixty-one-year-old grandmother, called to ask about enrolling in one of my anger management classes. After acknowledging that she spent the better part of every day being angry with her husband, she wanted to know how she could get him "to come with me to your class. He's the one that makes me *so* angry. I need to get him to change." I knew right away that Sally was codependent. *He* needed to change, but *he* was resistive, which left her angry and unhappy. Their marriage had been this way for twenty-seven years. I told Sally to forget her husband and come to the class alone. I appealed to her, "Do this for yourself."

Sally, it turned out, was the most toxically angry person in the class. In a typical week, she became angry, mostly with her husband, three to five times daily. Her anger was always intense, between levels 7 and 10, and it lasted anywhere from two hours to more than a day. There was rarely a time during the day, it seemed, when Sally didn't find herself angry.

This pattern repeated itself for six consecutive weeks, while we covered topics such as stress, assertiveness, empathy, and substance abuse. During the seventh week, however, there was a remarkable change! Sally began the group by stating that she had "turned over a new leaf" after the previous week's discussion of codependency. She had heeded the advice of fellow group members to "forget what your husband wants or doesn't want to do all the time. If you want to go to the flea market and he doesn't, *you* go anyway. And quit trying to stop him from climbing on the roof and doing other things that you think are risky, because you think you'll have to be his sole caretaker if he has an accident. Tell him that if he falls and hurts himself, there are plenty of nurses that can care for him. You'll be busy living your life." More important, Sally acted on the advice, and suddenly, for the first time in years, she found she had no reason to be angry. She was free! Sally reported only one episode of

> It took me almost fifty years to learn to enjoy life without feeling guilty, but I'm there now!

mild (level 2) anger during the last four weeks the class met, and that lasted only for 5 or 10 minutes—a 95 percent reduction in toxic anger. Four months later, she remains anger-free.

"I get angry once in a while, but it doesn't stick with me," she admits. "Anger is unimportant to me now. It's just not worth my time." Sally and her husband get along better than ever. He suggests it is because "she pretty much does what she wants now and doesn't stay after me as much."

THE THREE R'S

1. Try to *recollect* who and what you wanted to be before you became so emeshed in other people's needs. If you've never addressed questions about your identity—"Who am I? What makes me a *unique* human being?"—maybe now is the time to start.
2. *Restructure* your life so that you are an active part of it. Be a player, not a spectator. It is your life we are talking about after all!
3. *Realize* that the only true control we have in life is self-control. It is the springboard to self-esteem!

EXERCISES

1. Take some "personal" time each day no matter what the circumstances. If twenty minutes is all you can allow yourself, then take that, and enjoy! Maybe sometime you'll take a whole day just for you.

3. Repeat all the exercises you found helpful in the earlier chapters. Think of this as an investment in your new, nonangry self. Self-esteem is a powerful antidote to toxic anger.

4. Take a minute and complete the following sentences *without any reference to other people:*

I want _____

I am _____

I can _____

I need _____

I feel _____

I believe _____

I care about _____

I like _____

I do _____

I have _____

I have always wanted to _____

I think _____

I act _____

I hope _____

I am happiest when _____

I feel relaxed when _____

What did you learn about your "independent" self? Is this a self you could eventually learn to love? Is it a strong self? Or does it need to be nurtured? Are you willing to become your own caretaker? That's the best way to resist codependency.

◆ ◆ ◆

Are you suffering from the toxic condition known as codependency? If so, indicate it on the Toxic Anger Checklist on page 50.

CHAPTER 18

THE KEYS TO SUCCESSFUL CHANGE

How few there are who have courage enough
to own their faults or resolution enough to mend them!
—Benjamin Franklin, *Poor Richard's Almanac*

When it comes to persistent and complex problems, changing your behavior is a difficult task at best, which is why the majority of people who attempt change unfortunately fail. For instance, two-thirds of cigarette smokers who try to quit smoking relapse within three months. Seventy-two percent of alcoholics who successfully complete a treatment program resume drinking within six months. Those who suffer from obesity usually succeed at first but subsequently fail at one diet after another and end up heavier.

Why is change so difficult? Are people just not motivated enough? Do they have too little support from family, friends, and coworkers? Are their efforts misdirected? That is, are they trying to change the wrong thing? Are the theories and techniques that guide their attempts at behavioral change wrong or ineffective? Although it is possible that such factors play some role in the failure to change (see Chapters 5 through 7), most often the answer lies elsewhere.

Thirty years of helping people change unwanted behavior has taught me that people usually do not succeed long term because they

- fail to allow themselves sufficient time to achieve lasting change
- fail to persevere in the face of adversity
- fail to deal with the complexity of problem behavior
- fail to maintain their efforts to the point at which change becomes automatic
- fail to reward themselves for "small" changes made en route to their ultimate goal
- fail to quantify their progress

Don't make these mistakes! You *will* succeed if you follow the six key principles outlined in the following sections:

PRINCIPLE 1 *PERMANENT CHANGE TAKES TIME*

Most of us are in too much of a hurry to achieve lasting behavioral change. Imagine thinking that twenty-eight days of sobriety and group meetings are sufficient to "cure" an adult alcoholic who has been drinking excessively since she was a teenager, or that a single session of hypnosis will make someone quit smoking after twenty-seven years. At the least, such expectations are dangerously naive.

As the saying goes, "old habits die hard." The more complex and long lasting the habit, the more this adage is true. Toxic anger is no exception. Many of you have struggled with anger in one way or another your whole life, starting out as ill-tempered children and ending up as ill-tempered, hostile adults. Because invariably there are specific and highly individualized combinations of factors that predispose each person to maladaptive anger, each factor must be dealt with adequately before you can hope to conquer this burdensome problem. The more items you checked on the Toxic Anger Checklist, the more time you will need to allow yourself to succeed in a way that will have lasting benefit. I am suggesting here that you be both patient and realistic.

PRINCIPLE 2 *PERSIST AND PERSEVERE*

Because meaningful behavioral change takes time, it is important to continue making a committed effort every day whether or not you see evidence of immediate change in your emotional state. What you do on any given day is less important than the fact that you keep working at it over long periods of time. Focus on the effort, not the outcome; the latter will take care of itself.

Optimism helps! Studies have shown that an optimistic attitude ("something good will come of this") enables people to persist at things over time and, more important, to persevere in the face of setbacks and disappointments. Psychologist Christopher Peterson, in his book *Health and Optimism*, cites the example of varsity swimmers at a West Coast university who, after having completed a psychological questionnaire measuring optimism, were misled by the coaches into thinking that they had done poorly in their best event.[1] When they competed again, the pessimistic swimmers did even worse, whereas the optimistic swimmers markedly improved their performance.

People succeed as much from attitude as they do from ability. Attitude will certainly be crucial in your efforts to get beyond toxic anger. Reading this book will no doubt increase your ability to become a less angry person; the question is, Do you have the right attitude to see it through until the end?

PRINCIPLE 3 *WORK TOWARD CHANGE FROM A VARIETY OF FRONTS AT THE SAME TIME*

Do not limit your efforts to any one factor (e.g., stress, substance abuse, or maladaptive coping) now that you realize what needs to be changed. Instead, nibble away at the problem by working on several things simultaneously. This principle is important to remember because different

> My uncle John taught me to be resolute in everything I did in my life. As a child, whenever I said, "I can't . . . ," he would answer, "Son, *can't* never could." I never forgot that.

behaviors change at different rates. If depression is one source of your anger, it may take a considerable amount of time before your mood is significantly improved, for example, through the use of antidepressant medication. If this is the only element you are working on, you are likely to get discouraged and not persevere. However, if you are simultaneously learning to relax more, become a more assertive person, and exercise on a regular basis, you are likely to remain more hopeful that you can successfully reduce your toxic anger levels.

Start with your Toxic Anger Checklist. Go back to the chapters that deal with the factors you listed and make a composite list of selected exercises that can serve as a basis for long-term change. If you (like me!) checked most or all of the ten contributing factors, simply pick the three, four, or five you think influence your anger the most and construct a "recipe for anger change" out of these. You can always expand your efforts later on.

PRINCIPLE 4 *SUCCESS BUILDS ON ITSELF*

The maxim "nothing succeeds like success" perfectly illustrates this principle. In other words, success becomes addictive. If something works, we tend to repeat it. The toughest part of building toward sustained, permanent change, however, is forming a foundation of success from which we can continue to build over time. Once you begin to experience positive benefits from your efforts to change, continued efforts become less conscious and more automatic, or self-perpetuating. You quit thinking so much about making change and instead you "just do it!"

That is why, as I noted in principle 3, it is important to work on several fronts at once, so that you can form a "critical mass" of successful outcomes rather than waiting for success to come from one specific activity.

It is also important to remember that success comes as a direct result of the actions you are taking on your own behalf and not as a result of chance, fate, or sheer blind luck. The essence of behavioral self-help is that *you are both the problem and the solution*! It is all in your hands, to succeed or fail. Others provide support, but they cannot make you succeed.

PRINCIPLE 5 *IT IS IMPORTANT TO CELEBRATE SMALL VICTORIES*

In changing big problems, you most often experience small successes. For example, as you progress with your anger detoxification program, you may initially become angry just as often as you used to, but the intensity of your anger may be less or it may not last as long. This change *is* success, and you should celebrate! No question, this is a victory; see the glass as half full, not half empty!

Apply the same principle when you engage in the various exercises listed at the ends of the chapters. Celebrate each small step you take toward being more assertive, cutting back on anger-enhancing substances like alcohol and caffeine, or becoming more empathic. If this week you buy one of the books I recommend, then celebrate! If you sign up at a gym, then celebrate! If you switch to decaffeinated coffee, celebrate! If you drink two beers instead of the usual four, celebrate! All these changes count. They all add up. They all have meaning.

How do you celebrate? In two parts: (1) *acknowledge* that you have done something constructive, and (2) *reward* yourself with something tangible. Tell a member of your anger support team what you did and how good it made you feel. Don't be afraid to brag! Literally pat yourself on the back and say, "Good for me!" Treat yourself to a nice lunch or buy yourself some fresh flowers. Do whatever makes you feel special.

PRINCIPLE 6 *QUANTIFY YOUR PROGRESS*

Throughout this book, I have provided you with tools to measure various aspects of TAS: the three parameters of toxic anger, temperament, psychological and biological arousal, anger arousability, stress, passivity, and depression. Now use these tools to measure your progress each step along the way as you attempt to become a less angry person. Typically, you will find that the numbers change slowly, but progressively, step by step. For example, your TA summary score most likely will move down one level at a time, from 8 (extreme) to 4 (moderate), to 2 (mild), and eventually to 1 (nontoxic anger). The numbers themselves provide an incentive to continue with your program, and they also indicate when you should celebrate the gains you make along the way.

Quantification helps you avoid the trap of all-or-nothing thinking: "I'm either suffering from TAS or I am cured. There's no in between!" *There is always an "in between" where human behavior is concerned.* Quantification also reminds you that there is no quick fix. I rarely believe a client who tells me after four or five visits that "this stuff really works! Suddenly, I'm just not angry anymore." Unfortunately, *real* change isn't so immediate. Translated, the client is really saying, "I was hoping for a miracle, something that would change my emotional life instantly, with no real commitment on my part. And this seems to be it. Thanks. Bye." As you might guess, these clients all too soon discover they are experiencing the illusion of change, nothing more.

Remember, it is also wise to seek external verification that your assessment of your progress is accurate. Have a member of your anger support team fill out the questionnaires found in Chapters 3 and 4 each time you do, and then discuss any differences that arise.

How immediate and lasting are the effects of using the *Anger-Free*

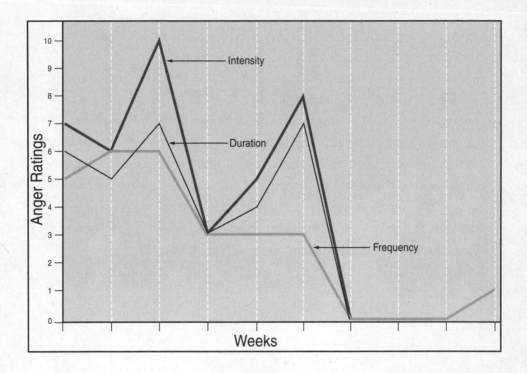

approach to problems of toxic anger? All the people I have worked with in our ten-week anger management classes—the format of which is identical to this book—showed a decrease in their anger ratings within the first few weeks. The figure above graphically illustrates a typical case. More important, these immediate effects persist over time, *if participants continue to follow the program*. Most people report a 70 to 75 percent reduction in anger at whatever point we contact them later on. One man, court ordered to our anger management classes for repeatedly assaulting his wife, put it this way: "I haven't had an angry outburst for months now. I've learned to control the things I can control and let the other stuff go. You were right; most problems in life really aren't the big deal I made them out to be." His wife, once a victim of toxic anger, echoed his sentiments: "I've been holding my breath, waiting for the anger to return, but I realize now that he's really changed. He really has."

Angry people tell us they like the concrete steps that the *Anger-Free* approach offers them. One said, "I left each class with a concept—for example, 'empathy is the only safeguard we have against rage'—that I could apply as soon as I got home." If you ask participants specifically for the key to controlling their anger, each one will give you a different answer. The effects are highly individualized, as are the causes of toxic anger. For some, the key to change is becoming more assertive ("It opened my eyes to what I was allowing other people to do to me"); for others, the crucial element is empathy ("I don't make as many assumptions about what motivates other people to act the way they do; instead, I try to put myself in their shoes"). One thing that *all* of our participants tell us is that they have a new, or renewed, sense of self-respect now that they have taken on the challenge of modifying their anger.

CHAPTER 19

THE CASE OF JOHN—REVISITED

He's much easier to live with now!
—John's wife

I began this book with a brief description of a very angry sixty-year-old man named John, who seemed to me, at the outset of our relationship, an ordinary man in all respects but one, his extraordinary temper. There was no question that John suffered from classic TAS and that he had done so for his entire adult life. The origins of his toxic anger could be traced to adverse childhood experiences that left him feeling socially alienated and always on the defensive. His anger, which his own family characterized as "vicious," invaded all aspects of his life. It made him physically ill, depressed, and embroiled in marital conflict; he lost friends, and he was unable to achieve the family intimacy he had longed for since childhood. But John wanted to change. He wanted a second chance at life, and he was willing to accept help.

I began working with John in 1987 and I have seen him a total of ninety-four hours. Although that may seem like a long time, it isn't considering how long he had suffered from TAS and the severity of his problem. Remember, meaningful change takes time!

Has he changed?

ASK HIM

John is quick to tell you that he is not the volatile, angry man he once was. When I first met him, he admitted becoming angry four to five times a day. Today, he can go weeks without experiencing anger. The average intensity of his anger previously was 9. Today, it is 3! His anger is over quickly as it always was. Situations that for all his life triggered uncontrollable, violent anger now only annoy him. As he put it, "Sometimes I might get a little peeved. But fly off the handle—no."

Much of his improvement comes from the fact that John has developed a less compulsive style for dealing with people and problems. He imposes fewer "shoulds, musts, have to's" both on himself and on those around him, and he is more intent on controlling his own emotions than on controlling the thoughts and actions of others. His views concerning why other people behave the way they do are less rigid and less accusatory ("What an idiot!"), and everything does not have to be so black-and-white. He is slowly learning to accept that people see life or feel things differently than he does and that they are not rejecting *him* just because they reject his *ideas*. He is much more empathic.

His psychological arousal (PA) score when I first met him was 54, which meant that he had a hair-trigger temper. Today, his PA score is 20, suggesting that he is less anger-prone than the average person. The most important lesson that John has learned through this process is this: "When I have a problem, I ask myself, 'What can I do about it?' If the answer is nothing, I let it go. I finally realized that the only thing I can control, for sure, is myself—my own actions, how I feel. So that's what I do."

John has lowered his biological arousal (BA) score as well. Initially, he scored +8 on the temperament scale. Today his BA score is +4. John is learning the value of relaxation and an active life outside of work. He is learning to rest when he is tired and to spend more time doing things he enjoys (he loves country music). His life is more balanced now.

If you've read this book from cover to cover, you know that John's story is my story, and the story of millions of other people. His success is my success—and it could be your success too.

ASK HIS WIFE

John's wife verifies John's tremendous change over the past several years. "You'd have to live with him like I have to really appreciate the difference—it's almost 100 percent!" she says. "He has definitely chilled out." On those infrequent occasions when he does get angry, it is very mild (level 1), more like annoyance.

When I asked her why she thinks John has changed after all these years, she said she wasn't sure. "I think maybe he finally realizes what he's got—his family, me," she guessed. "He seems to appreciate life more now." John talks to her more now about things that bother him. "He doesn't keep so much inside," she added. "We're closer than ever." He relaxes more too. "Before, he worked himself to death." Also, according to his wife, he has become less aggressive and more assertive. "Instead of ranting and raving like he used to, he just says no when he doesn't want to do something." John is also more empathic concerning his wife's health problems. "He used to get angry with me when I complained of pain; now he offers to help."

It is because John is no longer a toxically angry person that she concludes, "I think I'll keep him a while longer." It is obvious that she has always loved her husband, but for the first time in their forty years of marriage, she can relax and be her true self—say what she thinks, talk about her feelings, do what she wants—without always being afraid "he will take it the wrong way and get angry."

ASK HIS DAUGHTER

John's thirty-three-year-old daughter agrees that he is less angry now. The change for her, however, is less obvious than it is for John and his wife, partly because she no longer lives at home and is not around him as much. In addition, she shares his fiery temperament ("I hate to say it, but I am a lot like my dad"), and the two of them sometimes bring out the worst in one another when they get together. She loves her father, but she has not forgotten what it was like to be on the receiving end of his anger growing up. It is difficult for her to admit that he has changed as much as he has. "He thinks he was hard on us, but I don't think he realizes the degree of his anger," she says. "There are some things I'm sure he doesn't want to recall."

John's daughter concedes, however, that their relationship has vastly improved now that John's anger is under control. "He listens to me more now, and he's more open to my way of life. He's more tolerant, less judgmental," she adds. "He will even let me criticize him without blowing up. We have more of a dialogue now, whereas before I would always withdraw when he got so angry. We can actually sit down and have lengthy discussions about things, which we could never do before, not even two years ago." She enjoys her father's company now and makes a point of coming home to visit more frequently: "He's just more pleasant to be around." She no longer feels she has to be protective of her mother as she once did, now that her father is less angry, and she is becoming more interested in developing relationships with other men. Growing up around an angry father caused her "not to want any man ruling my life," but now that John has changed, so too have her attitudes about dating.

She says that John gets angry less often now and with more of a warning: "You can tell when it is coming, whereas before it was out of the blue. One minute you would think everything was fine, and the next minute it would be bad." Perhaps more important, her father's anger is much less intense now. "I must say he hasn't thrown anything in quite a while!"

Why did he change? "Because, I think, he is beginning to see that he was wrong," she says.

♦ ♦ ♦

Everyone agrees that John has been trying to change and that he has succeeded in his efforts. His wife attributes much of this to his therapy, but in fact John has done all the work. He was already motivated. Therapy simply provided him with the "tools," or the means by which to change— the tools that are described in this book. As John has changed, so has his family. It is a family that is slowly but surely "healing itself" now that John is anger-free. How do I see John and his family? As a work in progress.

♦ ♦ ♦

The fact that John, I, and the majority of the people described in this book have been able to free ourselves from the toxic anger syndrome means that you can change too. All you have to do is *make the choice today not to be angry tomorrow.* I hope you will.

Notes

Chapter 2: Toxic Anger Syndrome

1. C. Z. Stearns and P. N. Stearns, *Anger: The Struggle for Emotional Control in America's History* (Chicago: The University of Chicago Press, 1986).
2. P. Ekman and W. V. Friesen, "Constants Across Cultures in the Face and Emotion," *Journal of Personality and Social Psychology* 17 (1971): 124–129.
3. R. W. Novaco, "The Function and Regulation of the Arousal of Anger," *American Journal of Psychiatry* 133 (1976): 1124–1128.
4. W. D. Gentry et al., "Habitual Anger-Coping Styles. 1. Effect on Mean Blood Pressure and Risk for Essential Hypertension," *Psychosomatic Medicine* 44 (1982): 273–281.
5. J. R. Averill, *Anger and Aggression—An Essay on Emotion* (New York: Springer-Verlag, 1982), pp. 229–252.
6. C. D. Spielberger et al., "The Experience and Expression of Anger: Construction and Validation of an Anger Expression Scale," in *Anger and Hostility in Cardiovascular and Behavioral Disorders*, ed. M. Chesney and R. Rosenman (New York: Hemisphere, 1985), pp. 5–30.
7. J. R. Averill, "Studies of Anger and Aggression: Implications for Theories of Emotion," *American Psychologist* 38 (1983): 1145–1160.
8. Ibid (1982): pp. 176–182.
9. I. Kawachi et al., "A Prospective Study of Anger and Coronary Heart Disease. The Normative Aging Study," *Circulation* 94 (1996): 2090–2095.

Chapter 3: Self-assessment of Toxic Anger

1. J. R. Averill, *Anger and Aggression—An Essay on Emotion* (New York: Springer-Verlag, 1982).
2. M. E. P. Seligman, *What You Can Change & What You Can't* (New York: Alfred A. Knopf, 1994), pp. 127–128.
3. L. Madow, *Anger—How to Recognize and Cope with It* (New York: Charles Scribner's Sons, 1972), p. 4.

Chapter 4: The Angry Disposition: A Psychobiological Perspective

1. H. Selye, *The Stress of Life* (New York: McGraw-Hill, 1978).
2. W. B. Cannon, *The Wisdom of the Body* (New York: W. W. Norton, 1939).
3. R. W. Novaco, *Anger Control: The Development and Evaluation of an Experimental Treatment* (Lexington, Mass.: D. C. Heath, Lexington Books, 1975).
4. A. Bechara et al., "Deciding Advantageously Before Knowing the Advantageous Strategy," *Science* 275 (1997): 1293–1294.

5. A. Caspi et al., "Moving Against the World: Life-Course Patterns of Explosive Children," *Developmental Psychology* 23 (1987): 308–313.
6. A. H. Buss, *The Psychology of Aggression* (New York: John Wiley & Sons, 1961).
7. A. Caspi et al., "Continuities and Consequences of Interactional Styles Across the Life Course," *Journal of Personality* 57 (1989): 375–400.

Chapter 6: What's in It for Me?

1. J. Prochaska and C. DiClemente, *The Transtheoretical Approach to Therapy* (Chicago: The Dorsey Press, 1988).
2. E. DiGiuseppe et al., "Critical Issues in the Treatment of Anger," *Cognitive and Behavioral Practice* 1 (1994): 111–132.
3. T. I. Rubin, *The Angry Book* (New York: Collier, 1969).
4. D. T. Gianturco et al., "Personality Patterns and Life Stress in Ischemic Cerebrovascular Disease. 1. Psychiatric Findings," *Stroke* 5 (1974): 453–460.
5. I. Kawachi et al., "A Prospective Study of Anger and Coronary Heart Disease. The Normative Aging Study," *Circulation* 94 (1996): 2090–2205.
6. F. H. Gabbay et al., "Triggers of Myocardial Ischemia During Daily Life in Patients with Coronary Artery Disease: Physical Mental Activities, Anger and Smoking," *Journal of American College of Cardiology* 27 (1996): 585–592.
7. M. Friedman and D. Ulmer, *Treating Type A Behavior and Your Heart* (New York: Alfred A. Knopf, 1984).
8. H. H. Watkins, "Hypnosis and Smoking: A Five-Session Approach," *The International Journal of Clinical and Experimental Hypnosis* 24 (1976): 381–390.
9. E. I. Megargee, "The Dynamics of Aggression and Their Application to Cardiovascular Disorders," in *Anger and Hostility in Cardiovascular and Behavioral Disorders,* ed. M. Chesney and R. Rosenman (New York: Hemisphere, 1985), pp. 31–57.
10. A. Caspi et al., "Continuities and Consequences of Interactional Styles Across the Life Course," *Journal of Personality* 57 (1989): 375–406.
11. R. B. Williams et al., "Prognostic Importance of Social and Economic Resources Among Medically Treated Patients with Angiographically Documented Coronary Artery Disease," *Journal of the American Medical Association* 267 (1992): 520–524.

Chapter 7: Team Building

1. J. S. House, "Barriers to Work Stress: 1. Social Support," in *Behavioral Medicine: Work, Stress and Health,* ed. W. D. Gentry, H. Benson, and C. J. deWolff (Boston: Martinus Nijhoff, 1985), pp. 157–180.
2. "Sponsorship—What It's All About," pamphlet published by Al-Anon Family Group Headquarters Inc., New York, 1984.

Chapter 8: Mirror, Mirror on the Wall

1. T. I. Rubin, "Goodbye to Death and Celebration of Life," *Event* 2 (1981): 64.
2. M. Friedman and R. H. Rosenman, *Type A Behavior and Your Heart* (New York: Alfred A. Knopf, 1974).
3. V. A. Price, *Type A Behavior Pattern—A Model for Research and Practice* (New York: Academic Press, 1982).
4. A. Ellis, *Anger: How to Live With and Without It* (Secaucus, N.J.: Citadel Press, 1977).

Chapter 9: Give It a Rest

1. W. B. Cannon, "Stresses and Strains of Homeostasis," *The American Journal of the Medical Sciences* 189 (1935): 1–14.
2. T. H. Holmes and R. H. Rahe, "The Social Readjustment Rating Scale," *Journal of Psychosomatic Research* 11 (1967): 213–218.
3. P. J. Brantley et al., "A Daily Stress Inventory: Development, Reliability, and Validity," *Journal of Behavioral Medicine* 10 (1987): 61–74.
4. L. R. Gannon and L. Pardie, "The Importance of Chronicity and Controllability of Stress in the Context of Stress-Illness Relationships," *Journal of Behavioral Medicine* 12 (1989): 357–372.
5. R. Audrey, *The Social Contract* (New York: Antheneum, 1970).
6. H. Benson, *The Relaxation Response* (New York: William Morrow, 1975).
7. L. Eyre and R. Eyre, *Life Balance* (New York: Ballantine, 1987).
8. T. W. Graham et al., "Frequency of Church Attendance and Blood Pressure Elevation," *Journal of Behavioral Medicine* 1 (1978): 37–43.

Chapter 10: There's No Defense Like a Good Offense

1. C. D. Spielberger et al., "The Experience and Expression of Anger: Construction and Validation of an Anger Expression Scale," in *Anger and Hostility in Cardiovascular and Behavioral Disorders*, ed. M. Chesney and R. Rosenman (New York: Hemisphere, 1985), pp. 5–30.
2. J. R. Averill, "Studies of Anger and Aggression: Implications for Theories of Emotion," *American Psychologist* 38 (1983): 1145–1160.
3. W. D. Gentry and P. K. Kirwin, "Constriction, Aggression, and Assertive Training," *Psychological Reports* 30 (1972): 297–298.
4. S. A. Rathus, "A 30-Item Schedule for Assessing Assertive Behavior," *Behavior Therapy* 4 (1973): 398–406.
5. G. R. Bach and H. Goldberg, *Creative Aggression—The Art of Assertive Living* (New York: Avon Books, 1975).
6. T. Gaines et al., "The Effect of Descriptive Anger Expression, Insult, and No Feedback on Interpersonal Aggression, Hostility, and Empathy Motivation," *Genetic Psychology Monographs* 95 (1977): 349–367.

Chapter 11: Don't Fuel the Fire

1. E. H. Johnson, "Emotional and Familial Determinants of Smoking in Black and White Adolescents" (manuscript, University of Michigan Medical Center, Ann Arbor, 1989).
2. C. Ague, "Nicotine and Smoking: Effects Upon Subjective Changes in Mood," *Psychopharmacologia* 30 (1973): 323–328.
3. R. R. Hutchinson and G. S. Emley, "Effects of Nicotine on Avoidance, Conditioned Suppression, and Aggression Response Measures in Animals and Man," in *Smoking Behavior: Motives and Incentives*, ed. W. L. Dunn (Washington, D.C.: V. H. Winston, 1973), pp. 171–196.
4. H. H. Watkins, "Hypnosis and Smoking: A Five-Session Approach," *The International Journal of Clinical and Experimental Hypnosis* 24 (1976): 381–390.
5. S. Shiffman, "Relapse Following Smoking Cessation: A Situational Analysis," *Journal of Consulting and Clinical Psychology* 50 (1982): 71–86.
6. F. Clavel et al., "Nicotine Dependence and Secondary Effects of Smoking Cessation," *Journal of Behavioral Medicine* 10 (1987): 555–558.
7. D. R. Cherek et al., "Regular or Decaffeinated Coffee and Subsequent Human Aggressive Behavior," *Psychiatry Research* 11 (1984): 251–258.
8. P. E. Logue et al., "Effect of Alcohol Consumption on State Anxiety Changes in Male and Female Nonalcoholics," *American Journal of Psychiatry* 135 (1978): 1079–1081.
9. J. A. Borrill et al., "The Influence on Judgement of Facial Expressions of Emotion," *British Journal of Medical Psychology* 60 (1987): 71–77.
10. I. M. Bimbaum et al., "Alcohol and Sober Mood State in Female Social Drinkers," *Alcoholism: Clinical and Experimental Research* 7 (1983): 362–368.
11. J. Swanson, "Mental Disorder, Substance Abuse, and Community Violence: An Epidemiological Approach," in *Violence and Mental Disorder: Developments in Risk Assessment,* ed. J. Monahan and H. Steadman (Chicago: University of Chicago Press, 1994).
12. E. Harburg et al., "Negative Affect, Alcohol Consumption, and Hangover Symptoms Among Normal Drinkers in a Small Community," *Journal of Studies on Alcohol* 42 (1981): 998–1012.
13. J. M. Larson, *Seven Weeks to Sobriety* (New York: Fawcett, 1992).

Chapter 12: Walk in Their Shoes

1. A. D. Weisman, *The Coping Capacity—On the Nature of Being Mortal* (New York: Human Sciences Press, 1984).

Chapter 13: Exorcising

1. M. Friedman, *Type A Behavior: Its Diagnosis and Treatment* (New York: Plenum, 1996).

2. J. A. Blumental et al., "Effects of Exercise on the Type A (Coronary Prone) Behavior Pattern," *Psychosomatic Medicine* 42 (1980): 289–296.

Chapter 14: Avoiding the Black Hole

1. A. T. Beck et al., "An Inventory for Measuring Depression," *Archives of General Psychiatry* 4 (1961): 561–571.
2. A. L. Wesley et al., "Differentiation Between Somatic and Cognitive/Affective Components in Commonly Used Measurements of Depression in Patients with Chronic Low-Back Pain," *Spine* 16 (1990): S213–S215.
3. E. Zigler and M. Glick, "Is Paranoid Schizophrenia Really Camouflaged Depression?," *American Psychologist* 43 (1988): 284–290.
4. J. J. Ratey and C. Johnson, *Shadow Syndromes* (New York: Pantheon Books, 1997).
5. W. Styron, *Darkness Visible: A Memoir of Madness* (New York: Random House, 1990).

Chapter 15: If It's Broke, Fix It

1. A. D. Weisman, *The Coping Capacity: On the Nature of Being Mortal* (New York: Human Sciences Press, 1984).
2. A. G. Billings and R. H. Moos, "The Role of Coping Responses and Social Resources in Attenuating the Stress of Life Events," *Journal of Behavioral Medicine* 4 (1981): 139–158.
3. Ibid, Weisman, pp. 36–62.
4. A. Abel, *Don't Get Mad . . . Get Even* (New York: Norton, 1983).

Chapter 16: Read My Lips

1. J. W. Pennebaker, *Opening Up—The Healing Power of Expressing Emotions* (New York: Guilford, 1990).
2. J. W. Pennebaker, "Putting Stress into Words: Health, Linguistic, and Therapeutic Implications," *Behavior, Research & Therapy* 31 (1993): 539–548.
3. H. A. Kahn et al., "The Incidence of Hypertension and Associated Factors: The Israel Ischemic Heart Disease Study," *American Heart Journal* 84 (1972): 171–181.
4. A. W. Siegman et al., "The Angry Voice: Its Effects on the Experience of Anger and Cardiovascular Reactivity," *Psychosomatic Medicine* 52 (1990): 631–643.

Chapter 17: Taking Care of Number 1

1. M. Beattie, *Codependent No More* (New York: HarperCollins, 1987).

Chapter 18: The Keys to Successful Change

1. C. Peterson and L. M. Bossio, *Health and Optimism* (New York: The Free Press, 1991), pp. 122–123.

Index